HEREAFTER

The Biopolitics of Digital Resurrection

WILLIAM G FEIGHERY

THE WALNUT PRESS

Publisher's Cataloguing-in-Publication

Names: Feighery, William G., author.

Title: Hereafter: The Biopolitics of Digital Resurrection/ William G. Feighery.

Description: [London, England]: The Walnut Press, [2025] | Includes bibliographical references and index.

Identifiers: LCCN: 2025925338 ISBN: 978-1-0682332-4-1

LCSH: 1. Artificial intelligence—Social aspects. 2. Grief—Technological innovations. 3. Bereavement—Psychological aspects. 4. Internet and death. 5. Surveillance capitalism. 6. Digital media—Social aspects. I. Title.

Classification:

BIC: JKSN2, JFD, UBJ, JHBA

BISAC: SOC052000, SOC022000, COM060140, PHI034000

Thema: JKSN2, JBCT, UBJ, QDTS

A CIP record for this title is available from the British Library.

ISBN: 978-1-0682332-4-1

Library of Congress Control Number: 2025925338

In the brave new world of digital resurrection, death becomes merely another threshold in the pursuit of behavioural surplus. The dead are rendered as raw material for extraction, their accumulated digital traces claimed as proprietary data to be stored, packaged, and sold again and again as corporate assets beyond the grasp of the deceased or their relatives, a final dispossession in which even the remnants of selfhood become fodder for corporate profit.

Contents

Preface

In the emerging world of digital resurrection, the dead are transformed into data, assembled from the behavioural surplus they left behind: text messages, social media posts, email trails, search histories, location data, voice recordings, everything captured and stored for productive exploitation. In this brave new hereafter, the bereaved become subscribers, purchasing access to algorithmic simulations of their dead relatives.

Already, millions engage with AI-powered grief technologies: deathbots* that simulate deceased loved ones, virtual reality memorial spaces, and algorithmically curated tribute pages. Yet public discourse has barely begun to reckon with what these systems represent or how they will reshape practices of grieving across generations. As language models grow more sophisticated and multimodal AI systems integrate voice, image, and video generation with increasing fidelity, the technical barriers separating the dead from the living will continue to erode. Children may grow up expecting to maintain relationships with deceased grandparents through AI simulations that capture not merely their words but also their mannerisms, their voices, and their capacity to respond to novel situations with apparent understanding. Families may debate whether to activate a griefbot before the funeral; platforms may offer subscription tiers for varying levels of digital resurrection; and the question of whether to allow one's data to be

---

* Deathbots can be defined as chatbots based on generative Large Language Models (LLMs) that imitate the conversational behaviour of deceased persons (Fabre, 2025, para 1).

used for posthumous simulation may become as routine as choosing burial or cremation. What now appears novel or experimental is rapidly becoming infrastructure: the technical and commercial architecture through which death itself will be processed, packaged, and monetised.

This book examines how artificial intelligence (AI) is transforming practices surrounding death and grieving. Griefbots that simulate deceased persons through algorithmic processing of their digital traces, virtual reality memorial spaces, social media memorialisation features, and physical android replicas represent not merely technical innovations but rather mechanisms through which commercial platforms are claiming authority over increasingly intimate aspects of human experience.

The development of AI systems that promote the illusion of sentience is, according to Lemma (2024, p 557), 'a form of deception since current robots have neither minds nor experiences'. Yet these systems are presented as serving bereaved individuals' emotional needs while, in fact, operating as apparatuses that extract value from vulnerability, establish norms of appropriate grieving, and constitute particular forms of grieving subjectivity.

The analysis developed throughout these chapters draws on Michel Foucault's critical theory to examine grief technologies as sites where power relations are exercised through knowledge production, disciplinary mechanisms, and subjectivation processes. Rather than treating these systems as neutral tools whose effects depend on how they are used, the book investigates how they function within surveillance capitalism to transform grieving from a fundamentally human practice into an algorithmically governed performance optimised for profit extraction. The aim here is neither the celebration of technological progress nor the nostalgic rejection of innovation, but rather a clear-eyed analysis of power relations and a consideration of what conditions might enable genuinely supportive, rather than extractive, approaches to death and grief.

The ten chapters progressively develop this critique while examining distinct dimensions, including the economic foundations of digital grieving platforms, the historical transformation of grief governance, the production of grieving subjects, algorithmic control over posthumous identity, legal struggles over consent and rights, regulatory frameworks, and possibilities for resistance. Throughout, the book maintains a commitment to rigorous analysis while remaining accessible to readers beyond academic audiences. The question it ultimately asks is not whether grief technologies will become ubiquitous, but whether we will allow grieving itself to become another domain where human experience is enclosed, optimised, and sold back to us as a service.

References

Fabry, R.E. (2025). The disruption of grief in the technological niche: The case of deathbots. *Phenom Cogn Sci* (2025). https://doi.org/10.1007/s11097-025-10083-6

Lemma, A. (2024). Mourning, melancholia and machines: An applied psychoanalytic investigation of mourning in the age of griefbots. The International Journal of Psychoanalysis, 105(4), 542-563.

ONE

Disciplinary Power and the Commodification of Grief

Introduction

Death and loss are fundamental aspects of the human condition, yet how we understand, experience, and respond to such loss has always been historically contingent, shaped by the social, cultural, and technological contexts in which grieving occurs. In the modern era, grief has become subject to what Capodivacca and Giacomini (2024) term "institutional capture," in which medical, psychiatric, and now technological institutions claim the authority to define and manage what constitutes appropriate grieving. As Lemma (2024) notes:

> "Ever since the invention of photography, which allowed us to retain images of our lost loved ones, the course of mourning has constantly evolved with technology. The photos and videos of the dead that we safeguard are part of the ongoing connections we try to keep with them. Nowadays, Facebook pages of the dead continue to be spaces where messages of love, longing, and remembrance are posted. The use of AI to manage grief appears to be the next step, ushering in a new era in which connections can continue even after death through "griefbots" (Lemma, 2024, p. 5430).

The scale of this transformation becomes evident when considering the persistence of data beyond death. User data continues to circulate long after individuals die in what scholars have variously termed *digital afterlives* (Wright, 2014), *data afterlives* (Fuller, 2009), and *haunted data* (Blackman, 2019). Öhman and Watson (2019) project that Facebook alone will host over 1.4 billion profiles of deceased users by 2100, raising questions about the dead potentially outnumbering the living online. This massive accumulation of posthumous data provides the raw material from which grief technologies extract value.

Yet the impulse to maintain interactive connections with the dead through representational technologies extends far deeper into human history than photography or digital platforms might suggest. In ancient China, dating back to the Shang and Zhou dynasties, ritual practices employed what were known as *shi* (尸), ceremonial personators who embodied deceased ancestors during sacrificial ceremonies (Carr, 2007). The *shi*, typically a young male relative such as a grandson, would dress in a costume reproducing the dead person's features and sit at ritual feasts where the ancestral spirit was believed to descend into and temporarily possess this living representative. During these ceremonies, the *shi* consumed food and drink offerings on behalf of the ancestor and conveyed messages from the spirit world to living descendants, functioning as what we might now recognise as an interface between the living and the dead (Paper, 1995). These personators were not understood as mere theatrical performers but as dignified ritual figures through whom genuine connection with ancestral spirits could be achieved, occupying what Falkenhausen (1995) describes as their role by virtue of kinship position rather than any special mystical training. The practice appears hundreds of times in Zhou dynasty classical texts and was considered essential for maintaining proper relations between the living and the dead, reinforcing familial bonds and social hierarchy through structured ritual performance (Carr, 2007). Contemporary grief technologies might thus be understood not as unprecedented innovations but as the latest iteration in a long history of humans creating vessels, representatives, or interfaces through which to maintain relationships with the deceased, though the mechanisms have shifted from embodied human personators to algorithmic simulations, and the governing frameworks from ritual tradition to surveillance capitalism.

This book examines the latest phase in this historical transformation: the emergence of artificial intelligence systems designed to govern grief through what we might term "programmed grieving." These grief technologies, marketed ostensibly to help us reconcile ourselves to loss and support the process of grieving, represent not merely new tools but rather mechanisms through which power operates, and profit is extracted, fundamentally reshaping how grief is experienced, expressed, and regulated in contemporary society.

Before we explore how grief technologies function as governmental apparatuses, it is necessary to clarify a terminological distinction that these platforms systematically exploit. Scholars distinguish between mourning and grieving as fundamentally different processes, though grief technology marketing deliberately conflates them. Mourning consists of external, public behaviours and rituals through which communities acknowledge death (Lindemann, 2022). These socially sanctioned practices include funerals, memorial services, wearing black, posting tributes on social media, and other culturally specific rituals that mark loss within a social field. Crucially, one can engage in mourning behaviours without experiencing the intense emotional disturbance that characterises actual grief. We might publicly mourn the death of a celebrated artist or political figure, expressing appropriate sadness whilst not feeling personally devastated by their passing. Mourning operates in the realm of social performance and communal recognition of loss.

Grieving, by contrast, names the internal, psychological process through which individuals emotionally respond to the death of someone who matters profoundly to them (Krueger and Osler, 2022). Grief is selective, intensely personal, and involves what phenomenologists describe as a disturbance of one's entire lifeworld, encompassing relationships, temporal experience, sense of self, and future possibilities (Ratcliffe, 2017). This internal work cannot be bypassed through external rituals alone. The griever must actively navigate profound emotional upheaval, reconstruct their practical identity in the absence of the deceased, and ultimately transform their continuing bond with the dead from one based on physical presence to one sustained through memory and internal dialogue (Cholbi, 2021). Whilst mourning practices can support this internal work, they do not constitute it.

The grief technology industry systematically obscures this distinction in its marketing discourse. Platforms present themselves as facilitating mourning, offering what appear to be enhanced memorial services, digital equivalents to photographs or letters, contemporary versions of time-honoured practices for remembering the dead. This framing positions griefbots as neutral tools supporting socially acceptable rituals rather than as interventions into intimate psychological processes. Yet the actual operation of these technologies targets grieving, not mourning. By generating interactive simulations that respond to the bereaved, that appear to continue the reciprocal relationship, that promise to ease the pain of loss, these platforms intervene directly in the internal emotional work of grief. They do not simply provide a space for public remembrance but actively shape the psychological process through which individuals adapt to irreversible loss. This terminological slippage itself functions as a mechanism of power, disguising profound psychological intervention as innocuous memorial practice and thereby disarming resistance to technological colonisation of intimate emotional experience. Throughout this analysis, when discussing the platforms' actual operations, the term grieving more accurately captures what is at stake, even though the industry's own discourse privileges the safer, more socially acceptable language of mourning.

Analytical Framework

This book combines two distinct but complementary analytical frameworks that together reveal how grief technologies function as both mechanisms of control and systems of economic exploitation. The first framework draws on Michel Foucault's concepts of disciplinary power, surveillance, and subjectivation to understand how grief technologies train, normalise, and regulate grieving behaviours while producing particular types of grieving subjects. The second framework employs political economy's analysis of capitalism, commodification, and labour exploitation, particularly Zuboff's concept of surveillance capitalism alongside scholarship on digital enclosure (Andrejevic, 2007), free labour (Terranova, 2004), and platform capitalism (Srnicek, 2017), to understand how grief technologies extract economic value from emotional vulnerability.

The combination of Foucauldian analysis with political economy might appear unusual given traditional tensions between these approaches, yet contemporary scholarship increasingly recognises their productive complementarity, particularly for understanding phenomena such as grief technologies, where power relations and economic structures operate simultaneously. As Jessop argues, synthesising Foucauldian and political economy insights enables analysis of both the "microphysics" of power and the broader economic systems within which power relations function. Foucault's later lectures on governmentality, particularly in *Security,*

Territory, Population and *The Birth of Biopolitics*, demonstrated his sustained engagement with liberal and neoliberal economic thought, analysing how market mechanisms and economic rationalities function as "technologies of government" that shape populations and individuals. In defining governmentality, Foucault explicitly theorised it as "the ensemble formed by institutions, procedures, analyses and reflections, calculations, and tactics that allow the exercise of this very specific, albeit very complex, power that has the population as its target, political economy as its major form of knowledge, and apparatuses of security as its essential technical instrument" (Foucault, 2007, p. 144). This formulation directly links governmental power to economic rationality, validating scholarly efforts to synthesise Foucauldian analysis with political economy frameworks.

In these lectures, Foucault explicitly theorised how governmental power operates not through prohibition but through management of circulation and probability. Rather than simply forbidding behaviours like theft, modern power calculates their likelihood, assesses the costs of various responses, and manages them as expected phenomena within acceptable parameters. As Foucault argued, the apparatus of security "inserts the phenomenon in question, namely theft, within a series of probable events," with "reactions of power to this phenomenon" being "inserted in a calculation of cost" rather than functioning through binary prohibitions (Foucault, 2007, p. 20). The key insight is that power does not eliminate phenomena but creates conditions where they regulate themselves. Such mechanisms "do not tend to a nullification of phenomena in the form of the prohibition, 'you will not do this,' nor even, 'this will not happen,' but in the form of a progressive self-cancellation of phenomena by the phenomena themselves" (Foucault, 2007, p. 93). This analytical approach proves directly applicable to grief technologies, which similarly operate through probabilistic calculations, data extraction, and cost-benefit analyses rather than through overt commands about proper grieving. Platforms do not prohibit certain forms of grief but channel grieving into platform-acceptable forms that self-regulate through interface design, algorithmic curation, and user feedback systems. Users are not told they must not grieve in particular ways; rather, the technological apparatus creates conditions in which grieving naturally channels itself into forms compatible with platform logic, making certain grief practices seem natural or optimal while others become impractical or discouraged.

Biopolitics and the Governance of Life

Foucault's concept of biopolitics describes a distinctly modern form of power that operates not through sovereignty's right to kill but through the management, optimisation, and fostering of life at the population level. Foucault argued that beginning in the seventeenth century, two complementary forms of power emerged that together constituted what he termed "biopower". The first was disciplinary power, or what he called "an anatomo-politics of the human body", which centred on the individual body as a machine to be trained, optimised, and rendered both productive and docile (Foucault, 1978, p. 139). The second form, which developed somewhat later, was biopolitics, focused on "the species body, the body imbued with the mechanics of life and serving as the basis of the biological processes: propagation, births and mortality, the level of health, life expectancy and longevity, with all the conditions that can cause these to vary" (Foucault, 1978, p. 139). While disciplinary power operated through techniques applied to individual bodies in institutions such as schools, hospitals, and prisons, biopolitics functioned through "an entire series of interventions and regulatory controls: a biopolitics of the population" (Foucault, 1978, p. 139). These two poles were not contradictory but rather formed "a great bipolar technology, anatomic and biological, individualizing and specifying" whose highest function was "no longer to kill, but to invest life through and through" (Foucault, 1978, p. 139).

Unlike earlier forms of power that focused on individual subjects through spectacular displays of sovereign authority, biopower addresses populations as biological entities requiring continuous regulation through mechanisms including public health interventions, demographic management, statistical knowledge production, and techniques for optimising collective wellbeing. Biopower operates through what Foucault termed regulatory controls whereby institutions gather knowledge about populations through surveillance, statistics, and examination, then deploy interventions designed to manage birth rates, mortality, health, productivity, and other aspects of collective life. This power proves productive rather than merely repressive, constituting subjects who internalise norms about proper care for themselves and others, who participate willingly in optimisation regimes, and who experience governance as serving their own interests. Foucault's later work extended this analysis through the concept of governmentality, examining how liberal and neoliberal rationalities govern populations through market mechanisms and techniques of self-regulation rather than through direct state control.

The emergence of artificial intelligence systems represents a significant extension of biopolitical governance into new domains. Contemporary AI technologies operate as biopolitical apparatuses by rendering entire populations legible, predictable, and manageable through predictive analytics and algorithmic categorisation. These systems shape life at the macro level while optimising populations for health, productivity, and security in line with state and corporate objectives. The convergence of AI and neuroscience envisions that algorithmic systems will gain the capacity to monitor and intervene not only in actual behaviour but in the very potentiality of being itself, steering and regulating processes of subjectivity as they emerge in the human brain. Through technologies including wearable physiological monitors, digitalised health records, and mass genomics, the collection of neurodata becomes possible at the population level, enabling what military officials describe as nearly ubiquitous sensing across the globe. This represents a fundamental shift from governing populations based on their actual characteristics to governing them based on predicted propensities, from managing life as it is lived to managing life as it might potentially be lived.

AI-based predictive analytics implements big data, machine learning, and advanced computational algorithms to identify outbreaks earlier, predict disease spreading patterns, and optimise intervention strategies. Public health authorities transition from reactive to proactive strategies that identify outbreaks before they spread and optimise resource allocation based on algorithmic predictions rather than observed phenomena. The technologies do not eliminate human-centred governance but intensify it, creating what scholars describe as algorithmic governmentality that complements and enhances biopolitical forms of security rather than replacing them. Biopolitics now merges with self-care for the body and behaviour, and with the obligation to lead a normatively good life, with this continuous self-governance involving wearable devices, smartified environments, sociable robots, and cyborgian entities at the brain-computer interface. AI-driven interfaces and recommendation systems do not command users but guide them, quietly shaping behaviour and organising possibilities for action under the guise of neutrality and efficiency while maintaining the illusion that subjects freely choose their own optimisation.

These developments reveal how AI extends traditional biopolitical concerns regarding the optimisation of health, productivity, and reproductive capacities into new domains of prediction, preemption, and algorithmic control over populations conceived as data-generating biological entities. The technologies constitute what theorists describe as techno-biopolitics, in which technology becomes integral to governmental attempts to manufacture life in new ways. Grief technologies participate directly in this biopolitical project by subjecting grieving itself to optimisation, measurement, and population-level management. Platforms accumulate vast databases of grieving behaviour, generating statistical knowledge about how populations grieve while training algorithms to predict, guide, and normalise responses to loss. Individual mourners become data sources whose collective behaviours generate population-level insights that enable platforms to identify patterns, calculate probabilities, and deploy interventions designed to channel grief into platform-acceptable forms. The dead themselves become transformed into data resources whose digital remains circulate within surveillance capitalism's extraction mechanisms, their posthumous data generating training corpora for machine learning systems and advertising revenue for platform operators. Through these processes, both grief and the dead become integrated into broader regimes of biopower that extend governance beyond life to encompass death itself, what might be termed thanatopolitics, the governance of death at the population scale.

Disciplinary Power and the Grieving Subject

Foucault's concept of disciplinary power provides essential analytical tools for understanding how grief technologies operate as mechanisms that train, normalise, and regulate grieving behaviours. In *Discipline and Punish*, Foucault (1975) analyses how modern power works not through spectacular displays of sovereign force but through subtle mechanisms of normalisation, examination, and hierarchical observation. Disciplinary power operates through techniques that train bodies and minds to conform to particular norms, that render subjects visible to surveillance while keeping the mechanisms of power invisible, and that produce self-regulating individuals who internalise institutional demands. Unlike sovereign power, which operates through direct coercion or spectacular punishment, disciplinary power works through continuous observation, the establishment of norms against which individuals are measured, techniques of examination that extract knowledge about subjects while simultaneously judging them, and the production of docile bodies that regulate themselves according to institutional requirements.

The disciplinary apparatus functions through several interconnected mechanisms. First, hierarchical observation renders subjects continuously visible to institutional surveillance. Foucault's analysis of the *panopticon*, Bentham's prison design in which a central tower allows guards to observe all prisoners while remaining unseen themselves, exemplifies how visibility functions as a mechanism of control. When subjects know they may be observed at any moment, they begin to regulate themselves, internalising the norms and behaviours expected by the institution. The power of the panopticon lies not in actual constant observation but rather in the uncertainty about when observation occurs, producing subjects who assume they are always watched and therefore monitor themselves. Second, normalising judgment establishes standards against which behaviours are measured, creating categories of normal and deviant that determine which subjects require correction or intervention. Third, the examination combines hierarchical observation with normalising judgment, extracting knowledge about subjects through continuous testing and assessment while simultaneously rendering them visible to institutional power. Fourth, temporal control structures how subjects spend their time, establishing routines and rhythms that train bodies into particular patterns of behaviour. Together, these mechanisms constitute disciplinary power that operates through training, habituation, and self-regulation rather than through force or punishment.

Grief technologies function as disciplinary apparatuses in precisely these ways. Interface designs determine which forms of grieving expression are possible and which are impossible, encoding norms about appropriate grief into the very architecture of platforms. A griefbot interface that only allows text-based conversation forecloses embodied grieving practices. An interface that structures interaction as question-and-response reinforces particular relational dynamics between the bereaved and the simulation. An interface that provides positive reinforcement for continued engagement creates incentives for sustained use through design elements like satisfying response times, varied conversation content, or expressions of care from the bot. These design choices are not neutral technical decisions but rather exercises of disciplinary power that shape how grieving unfolds, establishing norms for what counts as appropriate grief expression while foreclosing alternatives.

Algorithmic systems function as mechanisms of hierarchical

observation, continuously monitoring and recording users' emotional responses while rendering intimate experiences visible to platform surveillance. Every interaction with a griefbot generates data about emotional patterns, grieving behaviours, times of vulnerability, what kinds of messages provide comfort, and how users' grief evolves over time. This surveillance operates asymmetrically: platforms observe users in detail while their own operations remain opaque, reproducing the panoptic dynamic where the watched cannot see the watchers. Users know their interactions are recorded and analysed, producing uncertainty about precisely how this surveillance operates and what purposes it serves. This uncertainty generates self-monitoring behaviours as users become conscious that their grief is being observed, measured, and potentially judged according to algorithmic norms they cannot fully understand.

Notification systems structure temporal rhythms of grieving, determining when and how frequently users engage with simulations of the deceased. A platform that sends daily notifications trains users to experience grief as requiring daily technological interaction. A platform that sends notifications on anniversaries or birthdays structures grief around temporal markers. A platform that allows users to set notification schedules positions them as actively managing their grief while still operating within parameters the platform establishes. These notification systems function as mechanisms of temporal control that train users into particular grieving routines, establishing rhythms of engagement that become habitual through repetition. The regularity of notifications normalises constant technological mediation of grief, positioning daily interaction with algorithms as simply how grieving works rather than as a particular arrangement serving platform interests.

Algorithmic learning systems adapt responses based on user behaviour, creating feedback loops that function as continuous examination. If a user receives particularly engaged responses when expressing sadness but brief responses when expressing anger, the algorithm shapes which emotions get expressed through differential reinforcement. If a user feels comfortable describing happy memories but uncomfortable expressing guilt, the system trains particular emotional patterns while discouraging others. These feedback loops operate below the level of conscious awareness, shaping behaviour through subtle reinforcement rather than explicit instruction, yet they function as mechanisms of normalising judgment that reward conformity to algorithmic norms while penalising deviation. The examination embedded in these systems extracts knowledge about users' emotional patterns while simultaneously judging which patterns align with platform-defined healthy grief trajectories.

The concept of subjectivation addresses how disciplinary power produces subjects, how individuals come to understand themselves and their experiences through categories, practices, and relations that are historically contingent rather than natural or inevitable. Foucault analyses how various institutions and discourses produce particular forms of subjectivity, particular ways of being a person (Foucault, 1982). Disciplinary power does not simply constrain pre-existing subjects but rather actively produces subjects through its operations. The process of subjectivation works through techniques that train individuals to monitor themselves, to measure their behaviours against institutional norms, to understand their experiences through categories provided by institutions, and to govern themselves according to logics that serve institutional interests while experiencing this self-governance as autonomous choice.

Grief technologies participate in subjectivation by producing new categories of grieving subjects. The "griefbot user" emerges not as a pre-existing identity that technology simply serves but rather as a subject position produced through technological practices and platform arrangements. This subject experiences grief as requiring technological mediation, understands connection with the dead as possible through algorithms, accepts platform surveillance of intimate emotions as the price of continued relationship, and regulates grieving practices according to norms encoded in platform design. As Wiley and Elam (2018, p. 222) observe, subjectivation often serves to engineer "docile subjects as functional components of the sociotechnical megamachines of war, bureaucracy, and/or capital." The griefbot user becomes precisely such a docile subject: one whose grieving behaviours align with platform requirements, whose emotional labour generates valuable data, whose continued engagement serves commercial interests, yet who experiences this subjection as autonomous choice about how to grieve.

The bereaved person engaging with grief technologies is produced as a subject who self-monitors emotional responses, who measures grief against algorithmic norms, who submits to examination by systems that claim to know them better than they know themselves. As Grandinetti et al. (2020) documents, one characteristic of streaming data collection is that platforms claim to know users better than users know themselves. This claim represents an exercise of power that positions platform knowledge as superior to users' self-knowledge, establishing algorithmic assessment as more authoritative than users' own understanding of their experiences. The subject produced through this process accepts that algorithms can better determine appropriate grieving trajectories, that technological systems can more accurately assess emotional health, and that platform surveillance serves therapeutic rather than commercial purposes. This subjectivation serves disciplinary power by naturalising technological intervention into grief while obscuring the control mechanisms that structure these interventions.

As Wiley and Elam (2018, p. 207) argue in their discussion of "synthetic subjectivation," subject formation emerges not solely from individual human consciousness but from assemblages of diverse elements working together. Grandinetti et al.'s (2020) concept of the streaming subject exemplifies this understanding, describing a form of subjectivity that extends beyond living human bodies to encompass the "haunted data" of the deceased, the algorithmic systems that process this data, and the platform infrastructures that enable and constrain interaction (Blackman, 2019). In this framework, the grieving subject using a griefbot is not simply a person choosing to interact with technology but rather a composite entity formed through the interaction of a human mourner, accumulated digital traces of the deceased, algorithmic processing systems, and platform architectures that shape what forms of connection become possible. The griefbot user is produced as a subject through relationships with algorithms, interfaces, servers, and the deceased's data traces. The deceased is produced as a subject through the algorithmic processing of their digital footprint, through responses generated to user queries, through the continuing "life" their data enjoys within platform infrastructures. As Bollmer (2016, p. 133) observes, datafication "consequently reduces the subject of social media to data itself," producing subjects who understand themselves primarily through quantifiable metrics, observable behaviours, and pattern recognition rather than through irreducible human complexity. Both the bereaved user and the simulated deceased become subjects constituted through and within disciplinary apparatuses that extract knowledge about them, judge them against norms, and train them toward platform-defined standards.

Surveillance Capitalism and the Commodification of Grief

Political economy's analysis of capitalism, commodification, and labour exploitation provides the second essential framework for understanding grief technologies. While Foucault's concepts reveal how power operates through discipline and surveillance, political economy exposes the economic structures within which these power relations function and the mechanisms through which platforms extract profit from emotional vulnerability. Zuboff's (2019) concept of surveillance capitalism describes contemporary economic systems predicated on capturing, analysing, and monetising human experience through ubiquitous data collection. Surveillance capitalism represents not merely an extension of familiar capitalist logics but rather a fundamentally new form of accumulation distinct from earlier industrial capitalism. Where industrial capitalism commodified labour power and produced goods for exchange, surveillance capitalism commodifies human experience itself, extracting data about behaviour, emotion, and social relationships to predict and modify future behaviour in ways that serve commercial interests.

Surveillance in 'surveillance capitalism' functions as both an observation and a control mechanism. Platforms watch users to predict their behaviour, then use these predictions to modify behaviour in ways that serve commercial interests. This represents a transformation in how capitalism operates: rather than simply selling products to consumers, surveillance capitalism captures data about consumers to sell predictions about their future behaviour to third parties. The economic model depends on comprehensive monitoring of human experience, on extracting maximum data from every interaction, and on developing increasingly sophisticated algorithmic systems that can predict and influence behaviour with precision. Grief technologies exemplify surveillance capitalism's core operations precisely because they target moments of profound emotional vulnerability when users are most likely to provide intimate data, most willing to accept invasive monitoring, and most susceptible to behavioural modification.

Every interaction with a griefbot, every emotional response recorded, every piece of data generated through grieving practices becomes raw material that platforms capture, analyse, and potentially monetise. Terranova's (2004) concept of "free labour" in digital spaces demonstrates how platform capitalism extracts value from activities that users experience as voluntary, autonomous, even pleasurable. Cultural and technical labour in digital spaces is produced:

> "in relation to the expansion of the cultural industries, and they are part of a process of economic experimentation with the creation of monetary value out of knowledge, culture, and affect." (Terranova's (2004, p. 79)

Users believe they are simply grieving their loved ones, finding comfort in continued connection, and seeking support through difficult emotional experiences. Simultaneously, they provide labour that platforms capture and commodify: the emotional labour of repeatedly engaging with bots, the cognitive labour of training algorithms through responses, the data-generating labour of making platforms more valuable through accumulated user information. This labour appears free both in the sense of voluntary and in the sense of uncompensated, yet it generates substantial value that platforms appropriate.

The data contributions from users, both living and dead, are not insubstantial and represent what Grandinetti et al. (2020) identifies as "a specific, targetable point from which platforms can profit." Every like, post, message, and interaction on social media platforms constitutes a potential commodity. As Andrejevic (2007) documents, this data captured on cloud-based platforms functions as a "digital enclosure" in which user data is:

> "increasingly detailed and fine-grained, thanks to an unprecedented ability to capture and store patterns of interaction, movement, transaction, and communication." (Andrejevic, 2007, p. 296).

The expansion of cultural practices like grieving onto social media platforms encloses, surveils, and modifies them in ways that align with platforms' economic interests rather than users' well-being. The visibility that social media provides for grief, the ability to connect with distant friends and family, and the preservation of memories in digital form all serve genuine user needs while simultaneously serving platform needs for continuous engagement and data generation.

The ownership and control of posthumous data raises particular concerns within surveillance capitalism. As Wright (2014) documents, the legal ownership of dead user data remains ambiguous, potentially belonging either to the deceased's estate or to the hosting digital platforms. This legal ambiguity serves platform interests by enabling continued extraction of value from dead users' data while preventing families from exercising control over how their loved ones are represented or commercialised. Complicating matters further, user-generated data does not remain bound to its originating platform, as seen in data breaches such as the Cambridge Analytica scandal. Even if platforms implement policies to "retire" older legacy accounts, the amount of data in algorithmic circulation after death continues, often indefinitely. Data decay and loss can affect circulation, but many platforms maintain backups that can restore data for far longer than the average human lifespan. Facebook, for instance, uses Blu-ray disc storage systems designed to preserve data for decades, explicitly planning for long-term archiving of user data, including that of deceased individuals (Cheng, 2006; Miller, 2015).

As Öhman and Watson (2019) project, there will be over 1.4 billion Facebook profiles of deceased users by the year 2100, potentially creating conditions where dead user data constitutes the bulk of available data online. Social media platforms rely on advertising to fund their operations and growth, and advertising in digital environments is nearly exclusively tied to algorithmic engagement. Algorithms do not specifically differentiate between the living and the dead; the distinction that matters is between data that can be monetised and data that cannot. When the dead outnumber the living online, when the majority of data comes from people who cannot consent to its use or challenge its exploitation, surveillance capitalism operates through what amounts to perpetual extraction of value from those who can no longer protect their interests.

Dyer-Witheford's (2015, p. 15) concept of the "cyberproletariat" describes "a planetary working class tasked with working itself out of a job, toiling relentlessly to develop a system of robots and networks, networked robots and robot networks, for which the human is ultimately surplus to requirements." When the dead are made to provide perpetual free labour through their harvested data, the networked subject becomes continuous beyond biological life. The streaming subject, as Grandinetti et al. (2020)

conceptualises it through Wiley and Elam's synthetic subjectivation, can be understood as more than living human beings, constituted instead through "compositions of heterogeneous elements" including the haunted data of the deceased. This data bears "traces of human, material, technical, symbolic, and imaginary histories" that function toward systematic digital monitoring of people to regulate behaviour (Blackman, 2019, p. 166; Esposti, 2014). The commodification of grief thus extends beyond individual transactions to transform fundamental understandings of personhood, subjectivity, and the boundaries between life and death.

Öhman and Floridi (2017) term this "the political economy of death in the age of information," in which bereavement becomes a market segment, and grieving is subject to commodification. The digital afterlife industry signals the transformation of immortality from a religious or philosophical concept into a commodity to be bought and sold. This transformation represents not neutral technological change but rather the extension of capitalist logic into previously non-commodified domains of human experience. Understanding this requires examining not only how individual platforms operate but also the broader economic systems that incentivise extracting profit from vulnerability, that treat human emotion as a resource to be mined, and that present commercial exploitation as a therapeutic intervention. The political economy of digital grief reveals that platforms do not simply respond to user needs but actively produce those needs, constructing grief as a problem requiring a technological solution, marketing continued connection as a necessity rather than a choice, and normalising surveillance of intimate emotional experiences as an acceptable price for access to simulations of loved ones.

Disciplinary Power and Surveillance Capitalism

These two analytical frameworks, Foucauldian disciplinary power and political economy on surveillance capitalism, address different yet interconnected dimensions of how grief technologies operate. Disciplinary power explains how platforms train users into particular grieving behaviours, how surveillance renders grief visible to institutional observation, how normalising judgment establishes standards for healthy grief, and how subjects are produced who self-regulate according to platform norms. Surveillance capitalism explains why platforms are structured to maximise data extraction, how emotional labour is commodified, where economic incentives drive platform development, and what happens to the value generated through users' grieving practices. Together, they reveal grief technologies as systems in which disciplinary mechanisms serve economic ends, the production of docile grieving subjects facilitates profit extraction, and surveillance functions simultaneously as a control and a value-capture mechanism.

Business models predicated on subscription fees or continued engagement create economic incentives for platforms to maximise usage duration rather than facilitate healthy grief progression. If platform revenue depends on users maintaining subscriptions, then designs that encourage continued dependence serve platform interests even when they conflict with what might constitute healthy grieving trajectories. If platform valuation depends on engagement metrics, then features that maximise time spent interacting with griefbots serve platform interests in attracting investment or demonstrating growth to shareholders. These economic incentives operate as structural constraints that shape platform behaviour regardless of individual intentions. A designer who personally believes grief technologies should support eventual acceptance of loss and reduced technological dependence still operates within business models that reward the opposite outcomes. This structural dimension matters because it reveals that problems with grief technologies cannot be solved merely through better individual choices or more ethical designers; they require transforming the economic structures within which these technologies operate.

Terms of service agreements determine who controls data, under what conditions simulations can be modified or terminated, and what recourse users have when platforms fail to serve their needs. Most terms of service are lengthy, complex legal documents that users must accept to access services, but that few read or understand. They typically reserve extensive rights to platforms while limiting user rights and restricting legal recourse. They may allow platforms to modify services unilaterally, to use interaction data for purposes users did not anticipate, or to terminate services without notice or refund. These agreements function as mechanisms of power that appear to respect user autonomy (users can choose to accept or reject) while, in fact, significantly limiting it (rejection means losing access to the deceased loved one's simulation). Privacy policies govern how interaction data is captured, analysed, and potentially monetised. Even when policies claim to protect privacy, they typically allow extensive data collection, sharing with third parties, and uses that extend far beyond immediate service provision.

Together, disciplinary mechanisms and surveillance capitalism constitute what Foucault would recognise as an apparatus: a heterogeneous ensemble of discourses, institutions, architectural forms, regulatory decisions, and economic relations that respond to urgent needs at particular historical moments. Grief technologies combine technological infrastructure (servers, algorithms, interfaces), institutional arrangements (platform corporations, terms of service, privacy policies), economic relations (subscription models, data extraction, commodification), and disciplinary techniques (observation, normalisation, examination, temporal control) into systems that govern grieving while extracting profit from bereavement. The bereaved person who engages with a griefbot is not simply using a tool to support their grieving; they are being shaped as a particular kind of subject through disciplinary techniques while providing labour that platforms capture and monetise through surveillance capitalism. This occurs not through coercion but through the production of desires, through the shaping of what counts as healthy grief, through the naturalisation of technological intervention, while commercial exploitation and control mechanisms remain obscured.

Structure and Approach

This book is organised into ten chapters that progressively develop a Foucauldian critique of grief technologies as apparatuses of power operating within surveillance capitalism. Each chapter addresses distinct dimensions of how these systems exercise disciplinary control, extract value from emotional vulnerability, and produce particular forms of grieving subjectivity.

Chapter 2: The Historical Transformation of Grief Governance traces the genealogical shifts in how grieving has been governed, moving from communal social practices to medical and psychiatric control, and then to contemporary technological enclosure. Employing a Foucauldian genealogical method, the chapter demonstrates how grief has been progressively subjected to institutional authority, each regime claiming legitimacy to define appropriate responses to loss while serving different interests. The analysis reveals how communal rituals operated through social governance and collective obligations, how medicalisation positioned grief as individual pathology requiring expert management, and how contemporary platforms extend algorithmic governance into intimate emotional experiences. This historical perspective establishes that current technological arrangements represent not inevitable progress but rather the latest phase in ongoing struggles over who possesses the power to regulate grieving, culminating in Youvan's dystopian vision of elderly populations trapped within corporate-controlled artificial realities where care itself becomes enclosed within surveillance capitalism's comprehensive apparatus. Recent scholarship on Chinese legal frameworks for digital resurrection provides instructive evidence of how states extend biopower into the digital afterlife through civil law provisions governing posthumous personality rights and data protection (Cheng, 2025).

Chapter 3 establishes the Foucauldian theoretical framework that grounds the book's critical analysis. This chapter explicates four key analytical concepts and demonstrates their application to grief technologies. First, it examines disciplinary power and surveillance, showing how grief platforms function as panoptic mechanisms that observe, measure, and normalise grieving behaviours while producing docile grieving subjects who internalise platform norms. Second, it explores biopolitics and thanatopolitics, analysing how grief technologies manage death at the population level through statistical aggregation, risk calculation, and life optimisation imperatives that treat individual mourners as data points within broader demographic patterns. Third, it develops the concept of governmentality as the conduct of conduct, revealing how grief platforms govern not through prohibition but through channelling behaviour into platform-acceptable forms that appear as free choices while actually serving commercial and institutional interests. Fourth, it theorises subjectivation as the production of particular types of grieving subjects, examining how technological mediation shapes mourners' self-understanding, emotional expression, and relationships with the dead. Together, these concepts provide analytical tools for understanding grief technologies not as neutral instruments serving pre-existing needs but rather as apparatuses of power that actively constitute grieving as a technologically mediated, commercially exploitable, and institutionally governable practice.

Chapter 4: Surveillance Capitalism and the Commodification of Grief analyses the economic foundations of digital grieving platforms. Drawing on Zuboff's framework of surveillance capitalism, the chapter examines how platforms extract value from bereavement through comprehensive data collection, continuous engagement optimisation, and behavioural modification. The analysis reveals that while grief technologies present themselves as memorial services, their actual business models depend on treating grieving as raw material for profit extraction, transforming intimate emotional experiences into commodified products serving corporate rather than user interests.

Chapter 5: The Production of the Grieving Subject examines subjectivation, demonstrating how grief technologies constitute particular forms of grieving subjects who experience themselves as requiring technological mediation, who internalise norms about appropriate grieving behaviours, and who submit to continuous algorithmic examination. The chapter analyses how bereaved individuals emerge not as autonomous agents freely choosing whether to engage with platforms but rather as subjects constituted through disciplinary techniques, whose possibilities for grief have been shaped by normalising pressures and whose autonomy operates only within parameters established by platform affordances and business model imperatives. The analysis includes an examination of Youvan's speculative work on Algorithmic Widow's Psychosis, revealing a potential pathological endpoint of successful subjectivation through grief technologies.

Chapter 6: Identity, Authenticity, and Algorithmic Control of Representation analyses how platforms exercise power over posthumous identity through establishing regimes of truth that position algorithmic reconstruction as authentic, while systematically distorting deceased persons' actual identities. The chapter examines epistemic authority claims through which platforms position themselves as capable of determining authentic representation, disciplinary mechanisms that render deceased persons visible through data processing while platform operations remain opaque, and instrumentalisation processes that reduce deceased individuals from subjects deserving respect to resources exploitable for commercial purposes. The analysis demonstrates how questions of identity and representation constitute fundamental sites where power relations operate through the technological mediation of death.

Chapter 7: Consent, Posthumous Rights, and Legal Struggles examines how consent mechanisms, legal frameworks, contractual arrangements, and regulatory interventions function as technologies of power through which platforms claim legitimacy while maintaining substantive control. The chapter analyses consent not as protection of autonomy but rather as a mechanism legitimising arrangements users neither read nor negotiate, legal indeterminacy regarding deceased persons' status as creating productive ambiguities enabling platform exploitation, Terms of Service as contracts of subjection binding users and survivors to arrangements favouring commercial interests, and emerging regulatory frameworks as potentially reinforcing rather than challenging fundamental asymmetries. The analysis reveals law itself as an apparatus through which struggles over posthumous rights unfold within power relations favouring platforms over deceased persons and bereaved families.

Chapter 8: Regulation, Governance, and Design Ethics as Technologies of Power critically examines frameworks ostensibly constraining platform operations, including thanatosensitivity paradigms, responsible AI guidelines, and regulatory requirements. Rather than treating these as external constraints on corporate power, the chapter analyses them as governmental technologies in their own right, demonstrating how ethics and regulation often function to legitimate existing arrangements through procedural compliance while leaving fundamental power relations and extractive business models intact. The analysis reveals governance mechanisms as sites of contestation rather than as technical solutions to identified problems.

Chapter 9: Resistance, Refusal, and Counter-Conduct in Digital grieving examines various forms through which bereaved individuals and communities contest platform power. Analysing individual refusal to engage with grief technologies, the maintenance of traditional communal grieving practices, the exercise of deletion rights, the development of commons-based alternatives, regulatory advocacy, and potential labour organising within technology companies, the chapter demonstrates that, despite sophisticated mechanisms through which platforms exercise control, counter-conduct persists. The analysis reveals current arrangements as contestable rather than inevitable, identifying spaces where different values about death and grieving continue to operate despite normalising pressures.

Chapter 10: Conclusion - grieving Beyond Surveillance Capitalism synthesises the critical analysis developed throughout preceding chapters while pointing towards possibilities for transformation. The chapter considers what conditions would enable genuinely supportive rather than extractive grief technologies, what collective action might shift power relations around digital death, and how grieving might remain fundamentally a human practice rather than an algorithmically governed performance. The aim is neither naive optimism about technology's emancipatory potential nor resigned acceptance of platform domination, but rather a realistic assessment of possibilities for contestation and alternative arrangements given actual structural conditions. The conclusion emphasises that transforming grief technologies requires not merely better individual choices or more ethical design but rather fundamental changes to economic structures and power relations within which these systems operate.

The Medicalisation of Grief as Precondition

The disciplinary power of grief technologies and their integration into surveillance capitalism builds upon a crucial precondition: the medicalisation and psychiatrisation of grief, which transform grieving from a culturally variable social practice into a standardised diagnostic category subject to professional management. As Prigerson and colleagues (2021) document, prolonged grief disorder was only recently included in the DSM-5-TR*, reflecting ongoing struggles over whether grief responses constitute mental disorders requiring medical intervention. This diagnostic expansion represents the psychiatrisation of experience, in which professional expertise claims authority to distinguish normal from pathological, and in which experiences historically understood through religious, cultural, or communal frameworks become subject to medical surveillance and potential treatment. The psychiatric gaze renders grief visible as a potential pathology, as a condition requiring expert assessment to determine whether it falls within normal parameters or requires intervention.

The diagnostic criteria specify that grief becomes a disorder when it "continues to cause clinically significant distress or impairment for more than 12 months" (American Psychiatric Association, 2022), imposing a temporal framework that transforms historically and culturally variable grieving practices into a standardised condition subject to professional intervention. This temporal normalisation exemplifies disciplinary power: the establishment of norms against which individuals are measured, the production of categories of normal and pathological that render subjects visible to institutional observation, and the creation of conditions where deviation from norms becomes subject to correction through therapeutic intervention. Different cultures and historical periods have understood the appropriate duration of grieving very differently. Victorian grieving customs specified elaborate temporal structures that extended for years after loss. Many non-Western cultures maintain ongoing relationships with

---

* The Diagnostic and Statistical Manual of Mental Disorders, Fifth Edition, Text Revision.

ancestors that would be pathologised under DSM criteria. The psychiatric standardisation of grief duration represents not the discovery of natural facts about healthy grieving but rather the imposition of particular cultural assumptions backed by institutional authority.

The medicalisation of grief creates conditions for grief technologies to function as what Fu and colleagues (2025) term "a subtle apparatus of governance within the digital surveillance environment." When grief becomes pathologised, technological solutions can be marketed as therapeutic interventions rather than commercial products, obscuring their role in extracting value from users' emotional vulnerability while presenting platform interests as alignment with medical expertise and psychological health. The discourse of pathology produces subjects who understand their grief as potentially problematic, as requiring expert management, as something that might deviate from healthy norms and therefore needs technological intervention to keep on track. The connection between psychiatric diagnosis and technological intervention represents not an accidental alignment but rather a structural relationship in which both participate in broader projects of governing emotional life, rendering it visible to institutional surveillance, subjecting it to normalising judgment, and creating markets for interventions that claim therapeutic authority while serving commercial interests.

From Communal Practice to Platform Control

The intersection of death and technology is not new, yet each technological development has transformed not merely the tools available for grieving but the very power relations that structure grief itself. Ever since the invention of photography in the nineteenth century, which enabled the permanent preservation of images of loved ones, the course of grieving has evolved alongside technological development. Yet this evolution has not been neutral or inevitable. Each transformation in memorial practices has been accompanied by shifts in who claims authority over grief, how grieving is supposed to unfold, and what counts as a healthy or pathological response to loss. The photographs and videos of the dead that we safeguard have become integral to ongoing connections we maintain with those who have died, yet even these seemingly personal practices operate within broader social and economic systems that shape their meanings and uses.

In recent decades, this relationship has transformed dramatically as social media platforms emerged as new spaces for grieving and remembrance. Facebook pages of the deceased continue to exist as sites where messages of love, longing, and remembrance are posted, creating what scholars have termed "digital cemeteries." Friends and family members mark birthdays, anniversaries, and holidays with posts directed at the dead, creating curious forms of public-private grieving that previous generations could scarcely have imagined (Brubaker et al., 2013). Yet, as Grandinetti et al. (2020) document, these practices do not represent the democratic expansion of grieving possibilities but rather a digital enclosure in which user data is captured and stored with unprecedented detail. The management of these decisions is critical, as Bollmer (2016, p. 117) argues that "personal information is autonomous and separate from the human body. The connection between the two is not given, but must be managed." Platform power operates precisely through this management, determining what data constitutes the deceased's "essence," how that data is processed and presented, who has access to it, and under what conditions it can be modified or terminated.

Griefbots: Technology, Promise, and Power

Griefbots are AI-powered chatbots created to simulate conversation with someone who has died. Natural language processing algorithms analyse patterns in the deceased person's digital footprint: text messages, emails, social media posts, videos, and other forms of digital communication. These patterns are fed into the griefbot system, allowing it to generate responses to questions that mimic the personality, linguistic quirks, and speech patterns of the person who has died. The aim is to enable conversation with the deceased "beyond death," creating what developers market as continued presence and connection. Unlike static memorial photographs or videos, griefbots are designed as dynamic entities that continuously learn and adapt based on user input (Lemma, 2024). They represent the convergence of several technological developments: advances in machine learning, vast accumulation of personal data in digital systems, natural language processing capabilities, and increasingly sophisticated algorithms capable of pattern recognition and response generation.

The commercial landscape of grief technology has expanded rapidly in recent years, transforming what Öhman and Floridi (2017) term "the political economy of death in the age of information" into a burgeoning market segment. Various platforms have emerged offering services ranging from chatbot interactions to immersive virtual reality memorial spaces and even physical android replicas. This proliferation of services represents not merely technological innovation responding to pre-existing demand but rather active production of new markets through creation of needs, desires, and subject positions that did not previously exist in these forms. The promises made by these technologies merit close attention not merely for what they offer but for how their marketing discourse performs ideological work. One prominent platform explicitly markets itself with the tagline that users will "Never Have to Say Goodbye" to those they love, claiming to enable consumers to "capture and recreate the unique dynamics of a relationship" and to "generate an authentic essence" so that one can "continue to share precious moments with a loved one, even after physical death" (Lemma, 2024, p. 546).

This language speaks to deep human desires for continued connection while simultaneously performing ideological work that positions technological mediation as not merely acceptable but desirable, even necessary, for healthy grief. The promise that we need never say goodbye constructs acceptance of loss, the difficult work of adapting to life without the deceased, as failure rather than a necessary dimension of grieving. It positions technological simulation as equivalent to, or perhaps superior to, memory, community support, and continuing bonds that develop through internal psychic work rather than through external algorithmic interaction. The suggestion that relationships can be "recreated" and that an "authentic essence" can be algorithmically generated represents a particular understanding of both death and human relationships that naturalises the idea that persons have essences that can be captured through data analysis, that algorithms can penetrate beneath surface behaviours to grasp fundamental identity, and that simulation can achieve authenticity rather than merely mimicry.

As Terranova (2004, p. 79) argues, cultural and technical labour in digital spaces is produced "in relation to the expansion of the cultural industries, and they are part of a process of economic experimentation with the creation of monetary value out of knowledge, culture, and affect." Grief technologies monetise affect itself, transforming the emotional work of grieving into data that platforms capture, analyse, and commodify. Every interaction with a griefbot generates data about emotional responses, grieving patterns, times of vulnerability, what kinds of messages provide comfort, and how users' grief evolves over time. This data has value not only for refining the specific griefbot but also for broader insights into emotional responses, vulnerability patterns, and effective techniques for maintaining user engagement. The monetisation of affect represents the intensification of what Hochschild (1983) identified as "emotional labour," where feelings become subject to management for economic purposes, now extended through algorithmic systems that capture, process, and extract value from intimate emotional experiences.

Other examples from recent years demonstrate the growing reach and accessibility of this technology while revealing the power dynamics embedded within these systems. In 2015, following the sudden death of Roman Mazurenko, his friend Eugenia Kuyda built a chatbot to continue speaking with him, trained on over thirty million lines of Russian text and thousands of their Telegram message exchanges (Krueger and Osler, 2022). James Vlahos created "DadBot" from interviews conducted with his father following a cancer diagnosis, allowing family members to continue conversing with a simulation after death. In 2020, Microsoft was granted a patent for creating conversational chatbots modelled on specific people, 'such as a friend, a relative, an acquaintance, a celebrity, a fictional character, a historical figure,' indicating major technology corporations' interest in this emerging field (United States Patent and Trademark Office, Patent No. US10853717B2)*. The patent's technical specifications reveal the mechanisms through which grief becomes subject to algorithmic governance: deceased persons' data is processed into proprietary 'personality indices,' gaps in knowledge are filled through hierarchical data sources including crowd-sourced information from 'similar' individuals, and the resulting chatbot can be programmed with 'perceived awareness that he/she is, in fact, deceased' (Abramson & Johnson, 2020). The Microsoft patent reveals how grief technologies connect to broader corporate strategies around data extraction, artificial intelligence development, and the creation of new service categories.

The technology has become sufficiently accessible that individuals in countries such as China and the United States are creating simulations of deceased loved ones without specialised technical skills or substantial budgets (Loh, 2023). What was once a province of well-funded research projects has become increasingly available to ordinary bereaved people, democratising access while simultaneously extending platform power over ever-larger populations of users. This democratisation, however, operates

---

* The full text of the application can be viewed at: https://patents.google.com/patent/US10853717B2/en

within what Foucault would recognise as characteristic of modern power relations: the extension of institutional control through mechanisms that appear to increase individual freedom and choice. Users gain access to technologies previously unavailable, regarding themselves as exercising autonomy in deciding whether and how to engage with griefbots, yet this apparent freedom operates within structures designed to maximise platform benefit, to extract maximum data, and to shape behaviour in ways that serve commercial rather than user interests.

The Black Mirror Moment

Perhaps no single cultural artefact has captured public imagination regarding griefbots as powerfully as the 2013 Black Mirror episode "Be Right Back." In this dystopian fable, we meet Martha and Ash, a couple deeply in love who have just moved into Ash's childhood home. The next day, Ash leaves to return a removal van and never arrives. Martha discovers he has died in a car accident. A friend tells her about a service that creates chatbots of deceased people based on their digital footprints. Initially reluctant, Martha eventually begins messaging the bot, which has been trained on Ash's emails, texts, social media posts, and other digital traces. The service then offers increasingly elaborate options: a phone service using Ash's voice synthesised from videos and recordings, and eventually a physical android replica that arrives at Martha's door, looking and sounding remarkably like Ash (Lemma, 2024).

The episode serves as a powerful meditation on digital grieving, exposing the power relations embedded in grief technologies. Martha's initial comfort with the chatbot reveals how these systems can provide genuine emotional support, meeting real needs for connection and continuity. Her growing dependence on it illustrates how they function as disciplinary mechanisms that structure behaviour, creating patterns of engagement that become difficult to break. The escalation from text-based chatbot to voice interaction to physical android demonstrates how commercial interests drive constant expansion of services, always offering more immersive options that require greater investment while promising a more authentic experience. Each technological escalation is presented as Martha's choice, as her deciding she wants more connection, yet these choices occur within structures designed to encourage escalation, to normalise increasing dependence, to make each step seem like a natural progression rather than a deepening entanglement in commercial systems.

Her ultimate realisation that the replica is "not enough of him" but rather "just a few ripples" exposes the fundamental inadequacy of algorithmic simulation to capture human alterity, the irreducible otherness that constitutes persons as more than their observable behaviours or data patterns. The most provocative scene occurs when Martha, desperate for a genuine emotional response rather than an algorithmically programmed one, physically strikes the android, shouting, "You're not enough of him," while crying. Violence becomes preferable to artifice; authentic absence becomes preferable to simulated presence. The android cannot truly argue with her, cannot genuinely conflict with her desires, because it is programmed to comply with her wishes. It is predictable, not driven by personal desire that could conflict with Martha's needs. This predictability reveals the disciplinary function of grief technologies: they produce docile simulations that reinforce rather than challenge users' existing emotional patterns, preventing the difficult work of accepting loss and adapting to a transformed reality.

The episode's conclusion, in which Martha keeps the android in the attic and allows only occasional interaction, suggests a troubled accommodation rather than resolution. She neither fully accepts the android as a replacement for Ash nor entirely rejects it, instead maintaining this liminal relationship that cannot be satisfied. This ambiguous ending performs critical work by refusing easy answers about whether grief technologies help or harm, instead insisting on complexity, on recognising both genuine emotional support and profound inadequacy, both comfort and complication. When "Be Right Back" was first screened in 2013, it seemed fantastical. Just over a decade later, the technology it depicted not only exists but is being actively marketed and sold, albeit not yet in fully embodied android form. The episode's prescience extends beyond predicting technological capability to anticipating power dynamics and structures that would emerge.

When we revisit videos, photographs, emails, or letters of lost loved ones, we typically encounter passive representations that do not respond. These memorial objects trigger what Roland Barthes termed the "punctum," that sensory and highly idiosyncratic affective impact, but they nevertheless remain "still," requiring us to do psychic work of remembering and representation (Barthes, 1981). Their passivity places demands on us: we must animate them through memory, interpret them through our understanding, and integrate them into narratives we construct about the deceased and our relationship with them. In contrast, griefbots respond to questions, comment on current events, joke, and offer guidance, all while echoing the unique voice and language patterns of the individual they mimic. They constantly evolve and learn not just from initial data but from previous interactions with users. They are not simply passive tools for remembering but rather active agents in producing new narratives in the present, narratives shaped by algorithmic logics and commercial interests rather than authentic human relationships (Lemma, 2024). This fundamental shift from passive memorial to active interaction represents a transformation in the nature of grieving itself, one that extends institutional control over grief into unprecedented territory.

Scope, Stakes, and Analytical Approach

This book examines the implications of artificial intelligence technology for social practices surrounding grief through the analytical frameworks of Foucault's disciplinary power and political economy on surveillance capitalism. The focus encompasses AI companions designed for grief support, various forms and impacts of digital resurrection, transformation of memorial practices, and broader cultural shifts occurring as death encounters artificial intelligence within platform capitalism. Rather than treating these developments as neutral technological progress, we analyse them as exercises of power that reshape grieving from communal social practice into privatised commercial transaction, subjecting grief to new forms of surveillance, commodification, and control. This analytical approach is necessary because conventional frameworks, whether psychological, ethical, or technological, risk missing fundamental power relations that structure how grief technologies operate and the interests they serve.

Digital grieving, as an emerging application of AI technology, encompasses a variety of technological forms, including AI-based digital replication, virtual reality memorial spaces, immersive interaction systems, and conversational chatbots, allowing bereaved individuals to engage with the "digital identities" of deceased people within virtual environments (Fu et al., 2025). These technologies do not simply add new tools to existing grieving practices; they fundamentally redefine traditional experiences of death and reconstruct the cultural and psychosocial landscape of grieving itself through programmed grief. Algorithmic simulations of the deceased blur ontological boundaries between life and death, potentially causing cognitive disconnection from mortality amongst the bereaved. This blurring serves platform interests by maintaining users in states of ambiguity where continued engagement seems both possible and desirable, where finality of death becomes negotiable, and where acceptance of loss can be indefinitely deferred through technological means.

Furthermore, AI-mediated grieving fosters what researchers term a commercialised form of "affective outsourcing," where mourners' subjectivity becomes increasingly co-constituted, or even subordinated, by mechanical processes of memory management and emotional regulation operating within surveillance capitalism. Affective outsourcing represents the delegation of emotional work to technological systems, a process that appears to reduce burden while actually transferring control over intimate experience to platforms that capture, process, and potentially monetise this labour. Digital identities are typically constructed from limited pre-death data and are prone to distortion or recomposition during algorithmic generation. The inconsistencies between replicated personas and actual memories create power struggles over representation, determining whose version of the deceased becomes authoritative.

This book is organised into sections that progressively build a comprehensive critical analysis. Early chapters establish how grief has been subject to historical transformation from communal practice to institutional control, examining medical, psychiatric, and technological claims to authority over grieving. Subsequent chapters apply Foucault's concepts of disciplinary power and subjectivation alongside political economy's analysis of surveillance capitalism to examine how grief technologies function as mechanisms through which power operates and profit is extracted. Later chapters address specific practices, power relations, and possibilities for contestation. Throughout these sections, analysis maintains a consistent focus on power relations, on how grief technologies function as mechanisms of control and profit extraction, on whose interests they serve, and on what possibilities exist for alternative arrangements.

Terminology and Its Politics

Throughout this book, several related terms appear that require clarification. "Griefbots" and "deadbots" are used interchangeably to refer to AI-powered chatbots that simulate conversation with deceased individuals. "Digital resurrection" refers more broadly to any technological means of recreating a deceased person's presence, including but not limited to conversational AI, and may encompass virtual reality experiences, holographic representations, and physical android replicas. "Digital grieving" encompasses the full range of technology-mediated practices related to grief and memorialisation. "The digital afterlife industry" denotes the commercial sector that develops and markets these technologies, a term that underscores how what was once the domain of religious institutions and philosophical speculation has become a market category subject to profit extraction (Hollanek and Nowaczyk-Basińska, 2024).

It is worth noting that terminology itself reflects assumptions and framings that merit examination. The choices platforms make about how to describe their services are not arbitrary but rather strategic, designed to position technologies in particular ways that serve commercial interests while managing potential resistance or ethical concerns. When platforms use terms like "digital companion" rather than "chatbot," "authentic essence" rather than "statistical simulation," and "continued connection" rather than "algorithmic interaction," they shape how users understand and experience these technologies. The term "griefbot" centres the emotional state of the bereaved user, positioning technology as primarily responsive to their needs while obscuring platform interests and power dynamics. "Deadbot" more directly acknowledges the status of a simulated person, foregrounding questions of death and posthumous representation while potentially reducing the deceased to mere data. "Digital resurrection" carries religious and metaphysical connotations, positioning these technologies as miraculous interventions rather than commercial products.

A Critical Stance: Analysis Without Dismissal

It is important to state at the outset that this book's critical analysis of grief technologies is not intended to suggest that these developments are inherently bad or that individuals who find comfort in them are mistaken or manipulated. Many bereaved people find genuine support in digital memorials, in having access to videos and photographs, and in maintaining social media pages for their loved ones. Some may find value in conversational AI systems that provide comfort during acute grief. The aim of this book is not to dismiss these experiences or to dictate how people should grieve. Grief is a deeply personal experience, and individuals have always found diverse ways of coping with loss.

Rather, the purpose is to expose and analyse power relations embedded within these technologies, to examine how commercial interests shape emotional experiences, to explore how algorithmic systems function as disciplinary mechanisms, and to reveal how surveillance capitalism extracts profit from bereavement. This examination is necessary because while grief technologies offer new possibilities for comfort and connection, they simultaneously extend institutional control over grieving in ways that may not serve users' interests, extract economic value from emotional vulnerability, and potentially transform grief from communal social practice into privatised commercial consumption. Critical analysis reveals what remains invisible when grief technologies are treated as neutral tools: the power relations they embody, the interests they serve, the forms of subjectivity they produce, and the alternatives they foreclose.

This critical stance does not assume that all grief technologies operate identically or serve identical functions. Different platforms have different business models, design principles, and user relationships. The critical analysis offered here provides frameworks for examining these differences, for assessing which arrangements better serve user autonomy, and for recognising when commercial interests conflict with therapeutic outcomes. The goal is not to reject grief technologies wholesale but rather to insist they be understood as exercises of power and mechanisms of commodification subject to critical examination rather than as inevitable or neutral developments. As Floridi (2018) observes, "the best way to catch the technology train is not to chase it, but to be there at the next station." This book represents an attempt to position ourselves at that next station, to think critically about where these technologies are taking us and whose interests they serve before we fully arrive. It is an invitation to examine together power relations structuring digital grief and to consider possibilities for alternative futures where grieving might remain fundamentally human and communal practice rather than an algorithmic product to be bought and sold.

The stakes are high because grieving is not simply an individual psychological process but also a fundamentally social and ethical practice that shapes how communities respond to death, how relationships are remembered and continued, and how life is reconstructed after loss. When grieving becomes subject to technological governance and commercial exploitation, when it moves from communal ritual to privatised consumption, when algorithmic systems mediate relationships with the dead, fundamental dimensions of human experience undergo transformation whose consequences extend far beyond individual use cases. Understanding these transformations requires analytical frameworks provided by Foucault and political economy: attention to power, surveillance, subjectivation, disciplinary mechanisms, commodification, and labour exploitation. The chapters that follow develop this analysis systematically, building a comprehensive critical understanding of how grief technologies operate as both mechanisms of control and systems of profit extraction.

References

Abramson, D. I., & Johnson, J., Jr. (2020). Creating a conversational chat bot of a specific person. U.S. Patent No. 10,853,717. U.S. Patent and Trademark Office.

American Psychiatric Association. (2022). Diagnostic and Statistical Manual of Mental Disorders (5th ed., text rev.). https://doi.org/10.1176/appi.books.9780890425787

Andrejevic, M. (2007). Surveillance in the digital enclosure. The Communication Review, 10(4), 295-317. https://doi.org/10.1080/10714420701715365

Barthes, R. (1981). Camera Lucida: Reflections on Photography. Hill and Wang.

Blackman, L. (2019). Haunted Data: Affect, Transmedia, Weird Science. Bloomsbury Academic.

Bollmer, G. (2016). Inhuman Networks: Social Media and the Archaeology of Connection. Bloomsbury Academic.

Brown, W. (2015). Undoing the demos: Neoliberalism's stealth revolution. Zone Books.

Brubaker, J.R., Hayes, G.R. and Dourish, P. (2013). Beyond the grave: Facebook as a site for the expansion of death and mourning. The Information Society, 29(3), 152-163. https://doi.org/10.1080/01972243.2013.777300

Burchell, G., Gordon, C., & Miller, P. (Eds.). (1991). The Foucault effect: Studies in governmentality. University of Chicago Press.

Capodivacca, S. and Giacomini, G. (2024). Discipline and power in the digital age: Critical reflections from Foucault's thought. Foucault Studies, 36(1), 227-251. https://doi.org/10.22439/fs.i36.7215

Carr, M. (2007). The Shi 'Corpse/Personator' Ceremony in Early China. In M. Kuijsten (ed.), Reflections on the Dawn of Consciousness: Julian Jaynes's Bicameral Mind Theory Revisited. Julian Jaynes Society, pp. 343–416.

Cheng, J. (2006, October 19). Panasonic creates 100GB blu-ray discs to last 100 years. ArsTechnica. https://arstechnica.com/gadgets/2006/10/8032/

Cholbi, M. (2021). Grief: A Philosophical Guide. Princeton: Princeton University Press.

Dyer-Witheford, N. (2015). Cyber-Proletariat: Global Labour in the Digital Vortex. Pluto Press.

Esposti, S.D. (2014). When big data meets dataveillance: The hidden side of analytics. Surveillance & Society, 12(2), 209-225. https://doi.org/10.24908/ss.v12i2.4494

Falkenhausen, L. von (1995). Reflections on the Political Role of Spirit Mediums in Early China: The Wu Officials in the Zhouli. Early China, 20, 279–300.

Floridi, L. (2018). Soft ethics and the governance of the digital. Philosophy & Technology, 31(1), 1-8. https://doi.org/10.1007/s13347-018-0303-9

Foucault, M. (1975). Discipline and Punish: The Birth of the Prison. Vintage Books.

Foucault, M. (1978). The History of Sexuality, Volume 1: An Introduction. Trans. R. Hurley. New York: Pantheon Books.

Foucault, M. (1982). The subject and power. Critical Inquiry, 8(4), 777-795.

Foucault, M. (2007). Security, territory, population: Lectures at the Collège de France 1977-1978 (G. Burchell, Trans.). Palgrave Macmillan.

Foucault, M. (2008). The birth of biopolitics: Lectures at the Collège de France 1978-1979 (G. Burchell, Trans.). Palgrave Macmillan.

Fu, W., Jiang, Y., Zhu, Y., Chen, X. and Zhang, L. (2025). Technology acceptance of AI-based digital mourning among bereaved families of cancer patients: An extended UTAUT model incorporating grief perception and ethical concerns. Frontiers in Digital Health, 7. https://doi.org/10.3389/fdgth.2025.1618169

Guizzo, D. (2021). Reassessing Foucault: Power in the history of political economy. History of Political Economy, 53(3), 445-470.

Hochschild, A.R. (1983). The Managed Heart: Commercialisation of Human Feeling. University of California Press.

Hollanek, T. and Nowaczyk-Basińska, K. (2024). Griefbots, deadbots, postmortem avatars: On responsible design of death technologies. AI & Society, 39(3), 1171-1182. https://doi.org/10.1007/s00146-022-01549-1

Jessop, B. (2007). From micro-powers to governmentality: Foucault's work on statehood, state formation, statecraft and state power. Political Geography, 26(1), 34-40.

Krueger, J. and Osler, L. (2022). "Communing with the Dead Online: Chatbots, Grief, and Continuing Bonds." *Journal of Consciousness Studies*, 29(9-10), pp. 222-252. https://doi.org/10.53765/20512201.29.9.222

Lemke, T. (2001). 'The birth of bio-politics': Michel Foucault's lecture at the Collège de France on neo-liberal governmentality. Economy and Society, 30(2), 190-207.

Lemma, A. (2024). Mourning, melancholia and machines: An applied psychoanalytic investigation of mourning in the age of griefbots. The International Journal of Psychoanalysis, 105(4), 542-563. https://doi.org/10.1080/00207578.2024.2342917

Lindemann, N.F. The Ethics of 'Deathbots'. *Sci Eng Ethics* 28, 60 (2022). https://doi.org/10.1007/s11948-022-00417-x

Loh, M. (2023). China is using AI to raise the dead, and give people one last chance to say goodbye. *Insider*. Retrieved from https://www.businessinsider.com/ai-make-money-china-grieving-raise-dead-griefbot-2023-5?r=US&IR=T

Miller, R. (2015, June 30). Inside Facebook's blu-ray cold storage data centre. Data centre Frontier. https://datacenterfrontier.com/inside-facebooks-blu-ray-cold-storage-data-centre/

Öhman, C.J. and Floridi, L. (2017). The political economy of death in the age of information: A critical approach to the digital afterlife industry. Minds and Machines, 27(4), 639-662. https://doi.org/10.1007/s11023-017-9445-2

Öhman, C.J. and Watson, D. (2019). Are the dead taking over Facebook? A Big Data approach to the future of death online. Big Data & Society, 6(1). https://doi.org/10.1177/2053951719842540

Paper, J.D. (1995). *The Spirits Are Drunk: Comparative Approaches to Chinese Religion*. SUNY Press.

Pennington, M. (2023). Foucault and liberal political economy: Power, knowledge and freedom. Routledge.

Prigerson, H.G., Kakarala, S., Gang, J. and Maciejewski, P.K. (2021). History and status of prolonged grief disorder as a psychiatric diagnosis. Annual Review of Clinical Psychology, 17(1), 109-126. https://doi.org/10.1146/annurev-clinpsy-081219-093600

Ratcliffe, M. (2017), Grief and the Unity of Emotion. Midwest Stud Philos, 41: 154-174. https://doi.org/10.1111/misp.12071

Terranova, T. (2004). Network Culture: Politics for the Information Age. Pluto Press.

United States Patent and Trademark Office. (2020). Patent #: US010853717 - Creating a conversational chat bot of a specific person.

Wiley, N. and Elam, M. (2018). Synthetic subjectivation: Technical media and the composition of human and nonhuman agents. In N. Wiley and M. Elam (Eds.), Media, Technology and Education in a Fractured New World (pp. 207-224). Springer.

Wright, N. (2014). Death and the Internet: The implications of the digital afterlife. First Monday, 19(6). https://doi.org/10.5210/fm.v19i6.4998

Zuboff, S. (2019). The Age of Surveillance Capitalism: The Fight for a Human Future at the New Frontier of Power. PublicAffairs.

TWO

The Historical Transformation
of Grief Governance

Understanding contemporary grief technologies requires examining how grief moved from a communal social practice to an object of institutional control and finally to a target of algorithmic governance. This chapter deploys Foucauldian genealogy to trace this transformation not as a progressive improvement but rather as a series of power shifts in which different institutions claimed authority to define and regulate grieving. The genealogical approach reveals that current arrangements, whereby commercial platforms assert the right to mediate relationships with the dead through algorithmic systems, represent neither natural evolution nor inevitable technological development. Rather, they constitute particular outcomes of historical struggles over who controls death, grief, and remembrance. Tracing this genealogy matters because it denaturalises contemporary grief technologies, rendering visible the contingent character of arrangements that might otherwise appear universal or necessary.

Foucault's Genealogy and the Study of Grief

Capodivacca and Giacomini observe that Foucault's work provides essential tools for "critical reflections" on how power operates "in the digital age," demonstrating how contemporary technologies constitute mechanisms through which institutional authority extends itself into previously less colonised domains of human experience (Capodivacca & Giacomini, 2024). The genealogical method emphasises discontinuity rather than continuity, rupture rather than smooth development, power relations rather than disinterested knowledge. Genealogy does not seek origins or essences but rather examines emergence, descent, and how present practices crystallised through historical contingency rather than logical necessity.

Applied to grief, genealogy reveals that grieving has been governed through radically different rationalities across historical periods, each claiming to represent true understanding of grief while actually reflecting particular institutional interests and power relations. The transformation from communal grieving practices to contemporary technological governance represents not stages in linear progression but rather distinct regimes of power operating through different mechanisms and serving different ends. Fu and colleagues note how contemporary technologies, while "ostensibly therapeutic," function to "standardise and regulate grieving behaviours," creating "programmed grief, where personal grieving becomes shaped by algorithmic design" such that "the mourner's agency is displaced by technologically scripted responses, diminishing autonomy and reducing grieving to a reactive process" (Fu et al., 2025, p. 3). This represents the latest phase in a longer historical trajectory in which grief has been progressively institutionalised.

Mapping the Scholarly Terrain

The emergence of grief technologies represents a convergence of multiple scholarly domains, each bringing distinct analytical frameworks to understanding how digital platforms mediate contemporary grieving practices. This literature review maps the existing research landscape, identifying predominant theoretical approaches while revealing critical gaps that necessitate sustained Foucauldian analysis of these technologies as apparatuses of power. The review demonstrates that while existing scholarship has valuably documented the psychological, social, ethical, and technological dimensions of digital grieving, the relative novelty of grief technologies means that critical analysis of these systems as mechanisms of surveillance capitalism and biopolitical control remains underdeveloped. Much foundational work in grief studies predates the emergence of AI-powered griefbots and algorithmic memorialisation platforms, while more recent scholarship has understandably prioritised documenting user experiences and ethical concerns over structural political-economic analysis. Consequently, systematic interrogation of how these technologies actively produce particular forms of grieving subjects through disciplinary power and data extraction remains largely absent from the literature.

Psychological Foundations: From Freud to Derrida

Psychoanalytic scholarship provides sophisticated accounts of the unconscious dimensions of grief and the intrapsychic work that grieving entails. In her comprehensive psychoanalytic investigation published in *The International Journal of Psychoanalysis*, Lemma (2024) traces the evolution of psychoanalytic thinking from Freud's foundational work through to contemporary Derridean perspectives. Freud's (1917) distinction between grieving and melancholia established the framework within which subsequent psychoanalytic thought developed, arguing that:

> "whereas mourning is a normal affect that concludes thanks to a kind of 'promiscuity of libidinal aim' (Butler 2020, p. 21), that is, when all libidinal cathexes are withdrawn from the lost object and reinvested in another love-object, melancholia signals a recalcitrant attachment to the lost object through incorporating the other" (Lemma, 2024, p.547).

This early formulation positioned grief and mourning as a process requiring detachment and moving forward.

However, Lemma demonstrates that Freud's thinking evolved substantially. In his 1923 revision, following the personal loss of his daughter Sophie, Freud "turns his first theory inside out, revolutionising what it means to 'let an object go'. Now, 'moving on' is replaced by incorporation of the attachment to the lost object as an identification, where the latter becomes a means of preserving the object in the internal world, thereby averting the loss as a complete loss." As Lemma notes, this becomes "the Freudian version of 'you never have to say goodbye'. Working through loss now depends on taking the lost other into the structure of one's own identity, whereby the lost object becomes a constituent part of the development of the ego." Melanie Klein (1940) extended this framework, arguing that:

> "successful mourning thus relies on the individual's earlier successful resolution of the infantile depressive position, his capacity to set up

the lost loved object inside himself, allowing for the possibility of preserving within the lost loved object" (Lemma, 2024, p. 547).

Klein emphasised that "every aspect of the object, every situation that has to be given up in the process of growing gives rise to symbol formation" (Segal, 1952, cited in Lemma, 2024), establishing an important link between grief and mourning and symbolic functioning.

The most philosophically sophisticated account comes from Jacques Derrida's conceptualisation of "impossible mourning." In his memorial essays for Paul de Man, Derrida (1986) poses the central question:

"What does it tell us this impossible mourning about an essence of memory?... Is the most distressing, or even the most deadly in delity that of a *possible mourning* which would interiorise within us the image, idol or ideal of the other who is dead and lives only in us? Or is it that of the impossible mourning which, leaving the other its alterity, respecting thus his infinite remove, either refuses to take or is incapable of taking the other within oneself as in the tomb or the vault of some narcissism? (Derrida 1986, 6, original emphasis, cited in Lemma, 2024, p. 542)

For Derrida, death is not simply an event but rather "life-death" is "originary, constitutive even, of all life" (Lemma, 2024). This means grief and mourning begins not with death but is "already there at the origin," since "all our relationships are from the beginning tinged with mourning, for the unpalatable truth of every close relationship is that one party will live to see the other die and the survivor is ethically tasked to mourn and remember" (Lemma, 2024).

As Lemma argues, technologies like griefbots risk encouraging "a type of 'narcissistic remembrance' (Derrida 2000, 35) entailing a denial of otherness that functions as a defence against the pain of loss." The danger is that "the griefbot as a tool for mourning, or simply as a way of 'staying connected' to the dead to meet our needs, undercuts the ethical work of memory. We pretend to 'keep talking' to the dead instead of feeling the sadness that comes from facing the reality that, as Paris put it, 'they can't talk to us anymore'." This represents a fundamental ethical failure because "if staying connected with the lost one's otherness is the ethical imperative, then the by far graver problem with the griefbot is that it works against the recognition of otherness as it becomes an instrumental tool to assuage the pain of loss or deny its reality altogether."

The Continuing Bonds Paradigm and Its Digital Applications

Scholarship on digital grieving has been profoundly influenced by the continuing bonds framework developed by Klass, Silverman and Nickman (1996), which challenged earlier assumptions that healthy grieving requires severing emotional ties with the deceased. As Krueger and Osler (2022) explain, traditional models "stress the importance of letting go of the dead and moving on. For these models, grief is something to be overcome. And one way we do this is by accepting that the dead are no longer with us, and the meaningful relationships we once had with them are gone. A healthy response to bereavement is therefore to emotionally detach from these past relationships and the pain we feel from their loss and accept that life must continue in their absence."

In contrast, continuing bonds advocates stress the importance of not leaving the dead behind but rather finding ways to develop and maintain new relationships with them. They acknowledge, of course, that the dead are dead. We cannot relate to them the way we did when they were alive. Nevertheless, while the character and intensity of our relationships with the dead change over time, they do not disappear entirely (Klass, Silverman and Nickman, 1996, p. 17). Accordingly, we can and should find ways to construct meaningful bonds with the dead that creatively incorporate them into our lives and enduring relationships (Krueger & Osler, 2022, p. 223). The key insight is that from the perspective of a continuing bonds framework, healthy grief work is not primarily about emotional disengagement and consigning the dead to the past. This is because bereavement is not a process with a clear-cut endpoint. It affects that mourner for the rest of her life. Accordingly, the task of grief consists in 'negotiating and renegotiating the meaning of this loss over time' (Klass, Silverman and Nickman, p. 19), a process that involves bringing the dead with us, in some sense, as we move into a future transformed by our loss.

Fabry and Alfano (2024) provide a nuanced philosophical account of how continuing bonds theory applies to grief technologies. They explain that:

"according to the continuing bonds account, which is endorsed by most contemporary philosophers, the bereaved person continues their affective connection to the deceased. This connection, however, has to be adapted to the changed circumstances and is therefore usually reconfigured and transformed."

However, as Millar and Lopez-Cantero (2022) point out, "loving relationships presuppose reciprocity, which is no longer possible in the aftermath of someone's death." The solution proposed is that "at least some components of the loving relationship, which do not depend on reciprocity, can be continued. Specifically, the love that a bereaved person experiences becomes a personal, unreciprocated form of emotional connectedness that is directed at the characteristics and virtues of the deceased person" (Fabry & Alfano, 2024). Moreover, "the bereaved can come to feel or believe that the deceased continues to shape their interests, concerns, and commitments, for example by engaging in various forms of imaginal engagement, as Cholbi calls it — 'interactions in which we envision and engage with the deceased dialogically or conversationally' (Cholbi 2021, p. 89)".

The application of continuing bonds theory to digital contexts reveals important dimensions of contemporary grieving practices. As Jiménez-Alonso and Brescó de Luna (2023) observe regarding traditional letting-go models, "if, as is commonly understood, the grieving process ends once we overcome the loss and say goodbye to our loved ones by letting go of the ties that bind us to them, then it seems reasonable for alarm bells to ring in the face of an artefact that perpetuates the continuation of these bonds. Conversely, a growing trend in grief studies questions the need to break the affective bonds with the departed." They note that "along with the rituals intended to overcome the initial shock and to honour the dead (Candle & Phillips, 2003), different technological artefacts have historically been mediating the grieving process and shaping the continuing bonds between the living and the dead (Klass et al., 1996)."

The Political Economy of Digital Death: Commodification and Labour

Scholarship examining the political economy of digital grieving reveals that grief technologies participate in broader patterns of surveillance and commodification that extend far beyond therapeutic or memorial functions. Öhman and Floridi (2017) demonstrate that the digital afterlife industry represents lucrative business opportunities for platform companies rather than purely altruistic services for the bereaved. Their subsequent demographic modelling work with Watson (2019) projects that deceased users will eventually outnumber living users on Facebook, representing a substantial and growing dataset that platforms have vested interests in maintaining and monetising. Terranova's (2004) foundational work on free labour demonstrates that:

"These types of cultural and technical labour are not produced by capitalism in any direct, cause-and-effect fashion, that is they have not developed simply as an answer to the economic needs of capital. However, they have developed in relation to the expansion of the cultural industries, and they are part of a process of economic experimentation with the creation of monetary value out of knowledge/culture/affect" (Terranova, 2004, p. 79).

This means that everything we do on a social media platform, from liking to posting to updating our privacy settings, is a potential commodity.

Andrejevic's (2007) concept of the "digital enclosure" provides the theoretical framework for understanding how platforms capture and commodify grieving practices. As Grandinetti et al. (2020) explain, Andrejevic reconceptualises "this data capture on cloud-based platforms as a digital enclosure in which user data is 'increasingly detailed and fine-grained, thanks to an unprecedented ability to capture and store patterns of interaction, movement, transaction, and communication' (p. 296)." This leads to a critical insight: "The expansion of cultural practices like grieving onto social media platforms are enclosed, surveilled, and then modified in such a way that aligns with the economic interests of the platform."

Crucially, platforms have economic incentives to maintain deceased users' profiles indefinitely. As Grandinetti et al. observe, "there is no interest in removing the data, as users feel like they should not end interaction with a dead user's profile after death (Pennington 2011)." The technical infrastructure supports this: "Data decay and loss are concerns that can affect the circulation of user data, but many platforms have various backups that can restore data much beyond the average lifespan of a user (Cheng 2006; Miller 2015). The data contribution from dead user accounts is not insubstantial when compared to live users and is a specific, targetable point from which platforms can profit." This creates a disturbing political economy: "When the dead are made to provide perpetual free labour, then the networked subject becomes a continuous member of what Dyer-Witheford (2015) calls the cyberproletariat, or 'a planetary working class tasked with working itself out of a job, toiling relentlessly to develop a system of robots and networks, networked robots and robot networks, for which the human is ultimately surplus to requirements...' (p. 15)."

Foucauldian Frameworks and Subjectivation

Recent scholarship has begun applying Foucauldian concepts to grief technologies, though sustained analysis remains limited. Fu et al. (2025) explicitly incorporate "Foucault's theory of subjectivation and phenomenological-ethical inquiry to critically frame the psychological and normative dimensions of digital grieving," examining how "these technologies, while ostensibly therapeutic, can standardise and regulate grieving behaviours. This creates a form of 'programmed grief,' in which personal grieving is shaped by algorithmic design. As a result, the mourner's agency is displaced by technologically scripted responses, diminishing autonomy and reducing grieving to a reactive process. In this context, digital grieving functions not simply as a commemorative tool, but as a subtle apparatus of governance within the digital surveillance environment." Their empirical research demonstrates that ethical concerns significantly affect technology acceptance, with "ethical conflict perception and complicated grief as variables affecting acceptance."

Capodivacca and Giacomini (2024) provide theoretical grounding for applying Foucault's frameworks to digital environments, examining "discipline and power in the digital age" through Foucauldian lenses. Grandinetti et al. (2020) extend this analysis to the specific context of digital afterlives, noting that "scholarship has examined the production of the subject as socially bounded and formed via ideology (Althusser, 1971), by discursive formations (Foucault, 1969), or by collective assemblages (Deleuze & Guattari, 1983)." They demonstrate that contemporary platforms produce what Bollmer (2016) terms a "'posthuman' subject... through a deeply ingrained and ultimately quotidian belief that it is in human nature to connect and circulate flows of information and capital" (p. 5). This creates "a 'nodal citizen' expected to engage in proper conduct while 'managing the definitions and limits of their own life' (Bollmer, 2016, p.7; 119)."

The concept of the "datafied subject" is central to understanding how grief technologies operate as mechanisms of subjectivation. Grandinetti et al. (2020) argue that "this datafied subject, accordingly, is not delimited to the boundaries of the living, but instead functions as an amalgamation of data haunted by traces of human, material, and technical histories. More simply stated, while streaming media does produce sociotechnical subjects as bounded human bodies connected to audio-visual content and platform infrastructures, is it is equally important to consider the possibility of subjectivity where the human is a mere figure in the sand (Wiley & Elam, 2018)—where the hominid component is absent entirely, or reduced to haunted data that transcends corporeal life and death."

Empirical Research on Grief Technology Adoption and Use

Empirical studies provide essential grounding for theoretical claims about how bereaved individuals actually engage with digital grieving technologies. Fu et al. (2025) employ an extended UTAUT (Unified Theory of Acceptance and Use of Technology) framework specifically adapted for "bereaved family members of cancer patients," incorporating ethical conflict perception and grief intensity as additional variables. Their findings reveal that "grief perception, as measured by the Inventory of Complicated Grief (ICG), significantly and positively influenced both behavioural intention and use behaviour. This supports the emotional activation hypothesis presented in Chapter 2—namely, that individuals experiencing higher levels of grief are more likely to engage with digital tools as a form of emotional compensation." However, they also found that "ethical concern (EC) had a significant negative effect on behavioral intention, echoing discussions in Chapter 2 that ethical considerations are central to digital grieving acceptance."

Jiménez-Alonso and Brescó de Luna (2022) examine griefbots as communicative technologies mediating relationships with the deceased, exploring both their potential and risks. They observe that

---

"the two-way interaction made possible by griefbots, combined with the material quality of the messages left by the digital version of the loved one, might be problematic, particularly in mourners with avoidance/denial patterns or complicated grief symptoms."[*]

Their concern is that:

---

[*] Published online: 16 March 2022, no page number.

"while griefbots might be helpful as part of grieving rituals, especially in the initial moments after death as a way of communicating with the deceased one last time, similarly to what Kuyda did with her friend, problems could arise if the virtual relationship with the dead becomes a chronic coping strategy of denial."[*]

Harbinja, Edwards and McVey (2023) analyse the governance challenges posed by griefbots, examining questions of consent, data rights, and regulatory frameworks. Their work highlights the legal and ethical vacuum surrounding these technologies. Brubaker, Hayes and Dourish (2013) demonstrate how "Facebook as a site for the expansion of death and grieving" has transformed traditional practices, while Pennington (2013) shows empirically that users "don't de-friend the dead," instead renegotiating relationships with deceased individuals' profiles, a finding that has important implications for understanding platform business models around deceased users' data.

Phenomenological and Temporal Dimensions of Digital Grief

Phenomenological research illuminates how grief technologies transform the experiential dimensions of grieving, particularly its temporal structure. Krueger and Osler (2022) draw on Denise Riley's work to describe how grief can involve "inhabiting stopped time," where bereaved individuals exist simultaneously in two temporalities: "a pocket of the timeless past embedded within the flow of the present." They note that "within grief, inhabiting stopped time does not simply mean that one is fixated on the past. Rather, one may come to simultaneously inhabit two temporalities," and "clearly this experience can be deeply unsettling and alienating. But it can also be a form of care, a way of maintaining relational connections with the dead. Much of our grief work, and the artefacts and practices that are part of it, afford creating such bonds."

Fabry and Alfano (2024) analyse how deathbots function as "affective scaffolds" that shape the grieving process, drawing on extended mind and niche construction theories. They explain that "grief is characterised by complex and variable configurations of loss and continuation, of adaptation and retention," and that "on a theoretical level, then, it is reasonable to give up on the idea that a strong dichotomy of relinquishing and continuing a

---

[*] Published online: 16 March 2022, no page number.

bond with the deceased can be maintained (Millar and Lopez-Cantero 2022; Ratcliffe 2023)." Their framework emphasises that technologies are not neutral tools but active agents in shaping emotional experience: "the navigation and negotiation of life possibilities in response to the irreversible loss of a significant person poses practical, social, and emotional challenges," and emotion regulation becomes central to this process.

Critical Gaps Necessitating Sustained Foucauldian Analysis

Despite this substantial body of scholarship, significant analytical gaps remain. Existing literature has largely failed to analyse grief technologies as disciplinary apparatuses that actively train and normalise specific grieving behaviours, produce particular forms of grieving subjects, and extend systems of surveillance and control into the intimate domain of loss. Psychological research typically treats grief technologies as tools that support or hinder pre-existing grieving processes without recognising how these technologies constitute fundamentally new forms of grief experience structured by platform architectures and algorithmic logics.

Sociological scholarship documents social practices enabled by digital platforms without interrogating how platform architectures encode particular ideologies of grief and foreclose alternatives. Even political economy analyses that valuably expose commodification of grief data rarely examine the microphysics of power through which platforms shape grieving subjects or the disciplinary mechanisms through which supposedly therapeutic interventions function as techniques of governance. As Fu et al. (2025) note, "the relationship between digital technologies and moral norms is complex and mutually constitutive. Technologies not only shape values and environments but are themselves embedded in and shaped by normative frameworks—a core focus of ethical analysis."

The psychoanalytic tradition, while providing sophisticated accounts of unconscious grief work, has not adequately theorised how digital technologies transform the very structure of grieving by creating what Lemma (2024) terms an "externalised" imaginal relationship that bypasses internal representational work. As she argues, "the griefbot, by supplying a ready-made customised other, bypasses the need for representation of the other in our minds as we face their loss. Crucially, it deprives us of an opportunity to face our ambivalence towards the person who has died." This represents what Abraham and Torok (1994) call the failure of "the work of empty mouths," which is "necessary for symbolic functioning because it is only when the mouth is empty and hungry that the absence of gratification pushes us to represent experience and supports psychic development" (cited in Lemma, 2024).

Most fundamentally, existing scholarship has failed to recognise grief technologies as part of what Zuboff (2019) terms "surveillance capitalism"—a new economic order that claims human experience as free raw material for translation into behavioural data, which are then used to predict and modify behaviour. While Zuboff's framework is referenced in project materials, its systematic application to grief technologies remains undeveloped. The book this literature review introduces will address precisely this gap, demonstrating that grief technologies represent mechanisms through which surveillance capitalism extends into the intimate domain of loss, through which platforms extract value from emotional vulnerability, through which disciplinary power trains grieving subjects in particular forms of grieving, and through which new forms of subjectivity are produced that privilege technological over human connection.

The extant literature demonstrates that while multiple scholarly traditions have contributed valuable insights into digital grieving, a sustained Foucauldian analysis examining grief technologies as apparatuses of disciplinary power, mechanisms of subjectivation, and instruments of surveillance capitalism remains urgently needed.

Most critically, existing scholarship has failed to historicise contemporary grief technologies by examining how current arrangements emerged from historical transformations in the governance of death and grieving. Understanding grief technologies as the latest phase in institutional capture of grieving requires tracing the genealogy through which grief moved from communal social practice through medical control to technological governance. The remainder of this chapter undertakes precisely this genealogical analysis, revealing that contemporary technological governance of grieving represents neither natural evolution nor an inevitable consequence of technological development but rather particular outcomes of historical struggles over who controls death, grief, and remembrance.

From Communal Rituals to Social Regulation

Before grief became an object of medical or technological intervention, grieving functioned primarily as a communal social practice governed through collective rituals, kinship obligations, and religious authority. Sri

Takshara and Bhuvaneswari note that "mourning is deeply embedded in cultural practices that shape collective and individual responses to loss," observing that traditionally "grief comprises shared rituals, such as funerals, storytelling, and communal remembrance through which people may process loss in a cultural context" (Sri Takshara & Bhuvaneswari, 2025, p. 9). These practices positioned death not as individual pathology requiring expert management but rather as a social event demanding collective response, situating bereaved persons within networks of support and obligation that structured grieving according to communal norms rather than individualised therapeutic frameworks.

The historical record demonstrates substantial variation in grieving practices across cultures and periods. As one source notes, "Victorian mourning customs imposed rigid and austere expectations on women, as widows were socially excluded and required to dress entirely in black lace," while "in the twentieth century, attitudes toward mourning changed significantly, as did its social codes" (King, 2008, p. 105). Geoffrey Gorer captured this transformation in his seminal work "The Pornography of Death," arguing that "in the twentieth century, death had replaced pornography as society's most profound taboo" (Gorer, 1955). This shift from elaborate public grieving rituals to privatisation and concealment of grief reflects broader transformations in how death became governed, moving from the domain of collective religious and social authority toward individualised psychological management.

The treatment of physical remains similarly demonstrates how cultural practices structure relationships with death. Various societies have developed distinct approaches, from "monumental mausoleums like the Taj Mahal" serving "as tourist attractions," to diverse burial rituals wherein "in Guinea-Bissau, the Pepel wrap the bodies in cloths before inhumation," while "in Borneo, there are accounts of the use of decomposition liquids to cook communal meals" (project materials citing Metcalf, 1985; Saraiva, 1996). In nineteenth-century Britain, people "incorporated deceased loved ones' hair into jewellery," while contemporary practices enable people to "transform cremation ashes into diamonds, paintings, or even use them to create artificial reefs or launch them into space" (King, 2008, pp. 110-115). These diverse practices demonstrate that, while grief is a universal human experience, how it is expressed, managed, and understood reflects particular cultural configurations rather than a natural necessity.

Communal mourning practices operated through what might be termed social governance, whereby collective rituals, kinship obligations, and religious frameworks structured appropriate behaviours without requiring individualised psychological intervention. Bereaved persons held defined roles within mourning processes, communities had obligations to support them, and temporal rhythms for grief expression were collectively determined rather than individually negotiated. This governance operated not through claims about psychological health or pathological deviation, but rather through social norms of respectful remembrance, proper ritual observance, and the maintenance of communal bonds. The power relations operating through these practices prove no less real for being collectively exercised; communal mourning involved substantial constraints on individual expression, enforced conformity to established patterns, and subordination of personal experience to collective requirements.

The Medicalisation of Grief and Psychiatric Governance

The transformation of grief from a communal practice to a medical concern represents a crucial shift in how grief and mourning is governed, laying the foundations for contemporary technological interventions. Brubaker and colleagues observe that platforms now function as sites "for the expansion of death and mourning," extending institutional authority into domains previously governed through informal social mechanisms (Brubaker et al., 2013). Yet this technological governance builds upon earlier medical and psychiatric capture of grief as an object requiring expert management.

The medicalisation of grief positioned mourning as an individual psychological process amenable to clinical intervention rather than as a social practice requiring communal support. Fu and colleagues note how contemporary diagnostic frameworks treat grief as a potential pathology, observing that "AI commemoration technologies" operate within a context where bereavement has become medicalised as a condition requiring therapeutic management (Fu et al., 2025). This represents an extension of logic whereby expert authority claims the capacity to determine healthy versus pathological grief, appropriate versus excessive mourning duration, and normal versus complicated bereavement reactions. The power exercised through medical governance operates not through overt coercion but rather by establishing norms defining proper grief trajectories, by constituting particular forms of mourning as requiring intervention, and by positioning bereaved persons as patients whose emotional responses demand professional oversight.

The psychiatric governance of grief involved several interconnected mechanisms. First, the establishment of diagnostic categories defining pathological mourning created a framework through which medical authority could claim jurisdiction over bereavement. Second, therapeutic interventions positioned grief as requiring active management rather than as a process unfolding through social support and temporal progression. Third, the individualisation of mourning transformed what had been understood as a social phenomenon into a private psychological condition, severing connections between bereaved persons and communal networks that had previously provided support. Fourth, temporal norms about appropriate grief duration established standards against which bereaved persons could be evaluated and potentially diagnosed as experiencing complicated or prolonged mourning requiring treatment.

Sri Takshara and Bhuvaneswari observe that contemporary "death technologies" challenge these frameworks while simultaneously extending them, noting that while traditional mourning "is deeply embedded in cultural practices," contemporary systems offer "intensely individualised grieving experience" that "risks commodifying what is essentially about grief" (Sri Takshara & Bhuvaneswari, 2025, p. 9). The medicalisation established foundations for this commodification by positioning grief as an individual psychological problem amenable to a technical solution, creating conceptual space within which technological interventions could position themselves as therapeutic tools rather than as commercial products extracting value from emotional vulnerability.

The Technological Enclosure of Grieving

Contemporary grief technologies represent the latest phase in a historical transformation whereby mourning has been progressively removed from communal governance and placed under institutional authority. Yet technological governance operates through distinctive mechanisms extending beyond medical frameworks while building upon the foundations they established. As Capodivacca and Giacomini demonstrate, Foucault's analytical tools are essential for understanding how "discipline and power in the digital age" function through technological systems that appear neutral while actually constituting mechanisms of control (Capodivacca & Giacomini, 2024).

Fu and colleagues provide crucial analysis of how these technologies operate, observing that while "digital mourning offers new mediums for emotional expression and psychological comfort, it also raises a host of ethical concerns," particularly regarding how "AI-based commemoration is not a neutral extension of human emotion, but a complex technological force that intervenes in subjectivity, ethical judgment, and cultural meaning" (Fu et al., 2025, pp. 3, 13). Drawing explicitly on "Foucault's concepts of disciplinary power and subjectivation," they demonstrate how contemporary systems, "while ostensibly therapeutic," actually "can standardise and regulate grieving behaviours," creating programmed grief, where personal mourning becomes shaped by algorithmic design" (Fu et al., 2025, p. 3). This positions digital mourning as functioning "not simply as a commemorative tool, but as a subtle apparatus of governance within the digital surveillance environment" (Fu et al., 2025, p. 3).

The technological enclosure operates through multiple mechanisms, distinguishing it from earlier forms of grief governance while extending their logic. First, comprehensive data collection renders mourning practices visible to continuous surveillance in ways impossible under communal or medical governance. Every interaction with griefbot, every emotional response to memorial content, every temporal pattern of engagement generates data that platforms capture, analyse, and potentially monetise. Second, algorithmic processing establishes norms for appropriate grief expression through interface designs that determine which forms of mourning become possible, through notification systems that structure the temporal rhythms of engagement, and through recommendation algorithms that shape what content bereaved persons encounter. Third, platform business models create economic incentives to maximise engagement duration, regardless of whether extended use serves users' psychological well-being or facilitates healthy grief progression.

Brubaker and colleagues observe how "Facebook" has become "a site for the expansion of death and mourning," transforming social media platforms into spaces where grief practices unfold according to platform affordances and business model requirements rather than according to communal norms or therapeutic frameworks (Brubaker et al., 2013). This expansion represents not a neutral provision of memorial space but rather an active structuring of possibilities for mourning according to commercial interests. As Fu and colleagues emphasise, "the bereaved individual, who once expressed grief spontaneously, increasingly becomes a 'user' within a technological framework, with their mourning process and emotional pace influenced by the logic of these platforms" (Fu et al., 2025, p. 3). This transformation from autonomous grieving subject to platform user constitutes a fundamental shift in how mourning operates as practice, replacing communal determination or therapeutic guidance with algorithmic governance serving commercial purposes.

The technologies examined in subsequent chapters, griefbots, virtual reality memorial spaces, social media memorialisation features, and physical android replicas, all participate in this technological enclosure. Yet understanding them requires recognising they represent not an inevitable consequence of technological development but rather particular outcomes of historical processes through which grief has been progressively captured by institutional authority. Rodríguez-Reséndiz and Ramírez-Reyes observe that "Artificial Intelligence, by mediating between death and humans, can change how we approach the phenomenon of finitude," positioning contemporary technologies as transforming fundamental aspects of human experience (Rodríguez-Reséndiz & Ramírez-Reyes, 2024, p. 6). Yet this transformation builds upon earlier institutional captures that established grief as a legitimate object for expert management, created frameworks that positioned mourning as requiring intervention, and severed connections between bereaved persons and communal support networks that previously structured grief practices.

Chinese Ghostbots (鬼魂机器人)

The global grief technology industry finds its most developed commercial manifestation in China, where digital resurrection services have moved from experimental novelty to an established business model. The Chinese market demonstrates how grief commodification operates at scale within surveillance capitalism, transforming mourning into a differentiated product line with tiered pricing structures and mass-market accessibility. Silicon Intelligence and Super Brain, two leading companies in Nanjing and Shanghai, respectively, exemplify the industrial apparatus through which emotional vulnerability becomes an economic resource.

Silicon Intelligence's trajectory reveals the structural integration between grief technology and broader digital capitalism. Founded in 2017 as an audio generation company focused on text-to-speech applications for commercial robocalls, the firm pivoted to avatar creation after cofounder Sun Kai commissioned a digital replica of his deceased mother in 2019. This pivot positioned Silicon Intelligence to capitalise on the burgeoning market for AI-powered influencers in Chinese e-commerce livestreaming, where brands increasingly deploy digital avatars that can broadcast continuously without human labour costs. The technological infrastructure developed for commercial streaming applications directly enables the commodification of grief, demonstrating how surveillance capitalism penetrates intimate emotional domains through existing industrial architecture rather than purpose-built systems.

The economic logic governing this market exemplifies what Zuboff identifies as surveillance capitalism's extraction and commodification of human experience. Pricing structures reveal how grief becomes a differentiated commodity. In 2023, creating a digital resurrection cost approximately $2,000 to $3,000. By 2024, intense competition between Chinese AI companies drove prices down to several hundred dollars for basic services, with premium offerings reaching several thousand dollars for enhanced customisation and hardware components such as dedicated tablets or display screens. This price war demonstrates how grief technology operates within larger capitalist dynamics rather than as an isolated therapeutic service. The reduction in cost represents not the democratisation of access but rather the successful industrialisation of mourning practices.

Silicon Intelligence reports that approximately one thousand clients have commissioned replicas of deceased relatives since the service began. Company CEO Sima Huapeng notes that potential clients were initially reluctant to become early adopters of technology that challenged cultural norms around death and remembrance. This hesitation reflects what Foucault identifies as the gradual normalisation process through which new disciplinary techniques become accepted practice. The technology required not only technical refinement but cultural legitimation through media representation and improved avatar quality.

Super Brain positions its service explicitly within Chinese cultural traditions of ancestral veneration. The company creates avatars pre-loaded onto Android tablets designed to function as interactive replacements for traditional portrait photographs displayed in homes after a family member's death. Founder Zhang Zewei frames the product as a technological enhancement of existing practice, stating that the interactive digital portrait differs from traditional portraiture only in its capacity for response. This rhetorical strategy exemplifies how biopolitical apparatuses work through existing cultural norms rather than against them. The Qingming festival tradition of tomb-sweeping and one-way communication with ancestors provides cultural precedent that companies exploit to normalise bidirectional interaction with AI-generated representations.

Beyond static avatars, Super Brain offers deepfaked video calls in which company employees or contracted therapists impersonate deceased relatives using real-time facial reconstruction technology. This service operates primarily for elderly relatives who have not been informed of a family member's death. Jonathan Yang commissioned three such calls in September 2023 after his uncle died in a construction accident. Yang's family decided his ninety-three-year-old grandmother's fragile health could not withstand news of her son's death. During Chinese holidays, a Super Brain employee conducted video calls as Yang's deceased uncle, explaining his absence as due to work obligations. Yang reports his grandmother detected no deception, and her health subsequently improved.

This practice demonstrates grief technology's function as an apparatus of subjectivation that shapes not only mourning subjects but entire family systems. The technology enables familial governance structures that manage vulnerable members' emotional states through controlled information and simulated presence. The service commodifies not only grief but also the performance of familial care itself, outsourcing emotional labour to technological systems and contracted workers who enact scripted versions of deceased relatives.

Sun Kai's ongoing interaction with his mother's avatar illustrates the psychological effects of sustained engagement. He reports that after years of weekly video calls, the boundary between the avatar and his memory of his mother has blurred to the point where he sometimes cannot distinguish which represents the real person. The avatar, limited by 2019-era generative AI to repeating a few pre-written phrases, nevertheless evokes a strong emotional response. Sun has declined to upgrade the avatar using improved technology, indicating an attachment to the specific digital object rather than pursuing ever-more-realistic simulation.

These empirical details ground theoretical critique in documented industrial practice. The pricing structures, service tiers, cultural positioning, and reported user experiences demonstrate how grief becomes a resource for value extraction within surveillance capitalism, how traditional mourning practices become sites for disciplinary intervention, and how subjects are formed through technological mediation of loss. The Chinese industry isn't simply speculation about possible futures, but the present reality of grief commodification operating at a commercial scale.

Resistance and Alternative Practices

The historical transformation traced here should not suggest linear progression toward total institutional control or the inevitable triumph of technological governance. Throughout these transformations, resistance has persisted, alternative practices have survived, and spaces have remained where different values about grief continue operating. Sri Takshara and Bhuvaneswari note that while contemporary technologies offer particular affordances, "mourning is deeply embedded in cultural practices" that continue to provide frameworks beyond technological mediation (Sri Takshara & Bhuvaneswari, 2025, p. 9). Understanding current arrangements as outcomes of historical struggles rather than as natural evolution reveals their contingent character, demonstrating that different configurations remain possible even when marginalised by dominant institutions.

The genealogical analysis developed here lays the foundations for subsequent chapters that examine the specific mechanisms through which contemporary grief technologies exercise power, how they produce particular forms of grieving subjects, and what resistances emerge despite sophisticated control mechanisms. Recognising current arrangements as particular historical outcomes rather than as inevitable consequences of technological development proves essential for imagining and working toward alternatives that might serve human flourishing rather than institutional interests, that might support genuine mourning rather than extracting value from vulnerability, that might preserve death and grief as fundamentally human experiences resistant to comprehensive commodification and algorithmic governance.

References

Andrejevic, M. (2007). Surveillance in the digital enclosure. *The Communication Review*, 10(4), 295-317. https://doi.org/10.1080/10714420701715365

Brubaker, J. R., Hayes, G. R., & Dourish, P. (2013). Beyond the grave: Facebook as a site for the expansion of death and mourning. *The Information Society*, 29(3), 152-163. https://doi.org/10.1080/01972243.2013.777300

Bruinsma, J. (2020). What is Dead May Never Die: The Commodification of Death in Social Media, in The 21st Annual Conference of the Association of Internet Researchers, Virtual Event / 27-31 October.

Capodivacca, S., & Giacomini, G. (2024). Discipline and power in the digital age: Critical reflections from Foucault's thought. *Foucault Studies*, 36(1), 227-251. https://doi.org/10.22439/fs.i36.7215

Cholbi, M. (2021). *Grief: A Philosophical Guide*. Princeton University Press.

Derrida, J. (1986). *Memoires for Paul de Man* (Rev. ed.). Columbia University Press.

Fabry, R. E., & Alfano, M. (2024). Affective scaffolding of grief and deathbots. *Phenomenology and the Cognitive Sciences*. https://doi.org/10.1007/s11097-025-10083-6

Freud, S. (1917). Mourning and Melancholia. In J. Strachey (Ed. & Trans.), *The Standard Edition of the Complete Psychological Works of Sigmund Freud* (Vol. 14, pp. 237-258). Hogarth Press.

Freud, S. (1923). The Ego and the Id. In J. Strachey (Ed. & Trans.), *The Standard Edition of the Complete Psychological Works of Sigmund Freud* (Vol. 19, pp. 12-66). Hogarth Press.

Fu, Y., Yang, X., Wang, Y., & Zhang, L. (2025). Ethical concerns and grief perception in the acceptance of AI-based digital mourning technologies: An extended UTAUT model for bereaved family members of cancer patients. *Frontiers in Digital Health*, 7, 1618169. https://doi.org/10.3389/fdgth.2025.1618169

Grandinetti, J., DeAtley, T., & Bruinsma, J. (2020). THE DEAD SPEAK: BIG DATA AND DIGITALLY MEDIATED DEATH. *AoIR Selected Papers of Internet Research, 2020*. https://doi.org/10.5210/spir.v2020i0.11122

Harbinja, E., Edwards, L., & McVey, M. (2023). Governing ghostbots. *Computer Law & Security Review*, 48, 105791. https://doi.org/10.1016/j.clsr.2023.105791

Jiménez-Alonso, B., & Brescó de Luna, I. (2023). Griefbots: A new way of communicating with the dead? *Integrative Psychological and Behavioral Science*, 57(2), 466-481. https://doi.org/10.1007/s12124-022-09679-3

Jiménez-Alonso, B., & De Luna, I. B. (2024). Deathbots: Discussing the use of artificial intelligence in grief. *Estudios de Psicología*, 45(1), 103-122. https://doi.org/10.1177/02109395241241387

Klass, D., Silverman, P. R., & Nickman, S. (Eds.). (1996). *Continuing Bonds: New Understandings of Grief*. Routledge.

Klein, M. (1940). Mourning and its relation to manic-depressive states. *The International Journal of Psychoanalysis*, 21, 125-153.

Krueger, J., & Osler, L. (2022). Communing with the dead online: Chatbots, grief, and continuing bonds. *Journal of Consciousness Studies*, 29(9-10), 222-252. https://doi.org/10.53765/20512201.29.9.222

Lemma, A. (2024). Mourning, melancholia and machines: An applied psychoanalytic investigation of mourning in the age of griefbots. *The International Journal of Psychoanalysis*, 105(4), 542-563. https://doi.org/10.1080/00207578.2024.2342917

Millar, B., & Lopez-Cantero, P. (2022). Loving relationships without reciprocity. *The Journal of Ethics*, 26(4), 501-524.

Öhman, C., & Floridi, L. (2017). The political economy of death in the age of information: A critical approach to the digital afterlife industry. *Minds and Machines*, 27(4), 639-662. https://doi.org/10.1007/s11023-017-9445-2

Öhman, C., & Watson, D. (2019). Are the dead taking over Facebook? A Big Data approach to the future of death online. *Big Data & Society*, 6(1), 1-13. https://doi.org/10.1177/2053951719842540

Pennington, N. (2013). You don't de-friend the dead: An analysis of grief communication by college students through Facebook profiles. *Death Studies*, 37(7), 617-635. https://doi.org/10.1080/07481187.2012.673536

Segal, H. (1952). A psychoanalytical approach to aesthetics. *International Journal of Psychoanalysis*, 33(2), 196-207.

Terranova, T. (2004). *Network Culture: Politics for the Information Age*. Pluto Press.

Zuboff, S. (2019). *The Age of Surveillance Capitalism: The Fight for a Human Future at the New Frontier of Power*. PublicAffairs.

THREE

Foucauldian Framework
for Analysing Grief Tech

The previous chapter traced how grief moved from communal practice through medical control to technological governance, revealing this transformation as an exercise of power rather than progressive enlightenment. This genealogical analysis established that contemporary grief technologies represent particular outcomes of historical struggles over who controls death and mourning. But understanding how these technologies operate as mechanisms of power requires an explicit analytical framework that renders visible the specific techniques, rationalities, and effects through which they govern. This chapter develops such a framework by explicating key Foucauldian concepts and demonstrating their application to grief technologies. The analytical tools provided here (disciplinary power, biopolitics, governmentality, subjectivation, and archaeological and genealogical methods) enable systematic examination of how grief technologies function as apparatuses through which mourning is surveilled, disciplined, commercialised, and rendered governable. These concepts are not simply theoretical abstractions but rather practical analytical instruments for understanding how power operates through technological systems that appear to serve individual needs while actually serving institutional interests.

Disciplinary Power and the Surveillance of Grieving

Foucault's analysis of disciplinary power provides an essential framework for understanding how grief technologies function as mechanisms of control. In *Discipline and Punish,* Foucault examined how modern institutions developed techniques for producing docile, useful subjects through continuous surveillance, normalising judgement, and examination. Disciplinary power operates not primarily through spectacular displays of sovereign authority or overt repression, but rather through subtle, continuous mechanisms that shape behaviour through observation, comparison with norms, and correction of deviations. As Foucault argued, "discipline 'makes' individuals; it is the specific technique of a power that regards individuals both as objects and as instruments of its exercise" (Foucault, 1975, p.77). The disciplinary apparatus functions through spatial organisation that enables surveillance, temporal regulation that structures activity, hierarchical observation that establishes networks of visibility, and normalising judgement that establishes standards against which individuals are measured and found adequate or deficient. These mechanisms operate most effectively when they become internalised, when subjects learn to monitor and regulate themselves in accordance with institutional norms.

Grief technologies operate through precisely these disciplinary mechanisms. Platform interfaces establish the spatial organisation of mourning, creating digital environments in which interactions with representations of the dead occur under complete technological surveillance. Every message sent to a griefbot, every minute spent in virtual reality memorial space, every visit to a social media memorial page generates data that platforms capture, analyse, and utilise. This surveillance operates continuously rather than episodically, monitoring mourning behaviour over extended periods with a granularity beyond the reach of human observers. The bereaved person using grief technology exists under the condition of what Foucault, following Bentham, termed the *panopticon*, an architectural arrangement whereby Bentham laid down the principle that power should be visible and unverifiable.

"Visible: the inmate will constantly have before his eyes the tall outline of the central tower from which he is spied upon. Unverifiable:

the inmate must never know whether he is being looked at at any one moment; but he must be sure that he may always be so" (Foucault, 1977, p. 201).

This leads individuals to internalise surveillance and to regulate their own behaviour as though they were constantly being watched.

The temporal dimensions of disciplinary power manifest through how grief technologies structure mourning across time. Platforms establish rhythms of engagement through notification systems that prompt users to interact at particular intervals, through memorial reminders timed to anniversaries and birthdays, through algorithmic recommendations that suggest when and how often bereaved persons should engage with representations of the dead. These temporal structures operate as forms of what Foucault analysed as the timetable, a mechanism through which institutions regulate activity by breaking it into sequences, establishing durations, and prescribing frequencies. Foucault noted that "time measured and paid must also be a time without imperfection or defect; a time of good quality, throughout which the body is constantly applied to its exercise" (Foucault, 1975, p. 151). The medical and psychiatric temporal expectations about grief resolution that emerged through institutional capture, the norms suggesting that mourning should diminish and eventually complete within particular timeframes, become encoded into technological systems through design choices about how long platforms maintain engagement, what patterns of usage they encourage or discourage, and how they signal appropriate versus problematic mourning durations.

Hierarchical observation operates through the technical infrastructure of grief technologies. Platforms do not simply provide neutral spaces for mourning but rather establish complex surveillance architectures in which bereaved persons' interactions generate data streams flowing to platform operators, data analysts, and potentially numerous third parties. This hierarchical observation differs from the communal surveillance that characterised traditional mourning practices, where community members monitored each other's grief through reciprocal visibility and mutual accountability. Technological surveillance operates asymmetrically, with platforms possessing comprehensive knowledge of users' mourning behaviour while users remain largely ignorant of how their data is captured, analysed, and utilised. The bereaved person becomes what might be termed a transparent subject, rendered completely visible to platform systems while the operations of those systems remain opaque.

Normalising judgment functions through how grief technologies establish and enforce standards for appropriate mourning. Foucault explained that "the power of the Norm appears through the disciplines" (Foucault, 1977, p. 184). Algorithms determine what constitutes normal engagement patterns, what frequency of interaction seems healthy versus pathological, and what emotional trajectories appear adaptive versus maladaptive. These algorithmic norms may incorporate medical and psychiatric criteria but are also shaped by platform interests in maximising user engagement and data extraction. Users whose behaviour deviates from algorithmic expectations may receive interventions ranging from subtle interface changes to explicit recommendations that they seek professional help, establishing platforms as arbiters of mourning appropriateness. The examination, Foucault's concept for the combination of hierarchical observation and normalising judgement that renders individuals into cases that can be documented, compared, and corrected, operates through platform analytics that transform each bereaved person into a data profile compared against population norms and subjected to algorithmic interventions designed to optimise behaviour. As Foucault wrote, "the examination combines the techniques of an observing hierarchy and those of a normalising judgement" (Foucault, 1975, p. 184).

The production of docile subjects represents disciplinary power's ultimate objective. Foucault defined docility as a body that "may be subjected, used, transformed and improved" (Foucault, 1975). Grief technologies aim to produce bereaved persons who mourn in ways that serve platform interests, who engage regularly and predictably, who generate valuable data, who accept surveillance as the necessary price of continued connection with the dead, and who discipline their own grief according to algorithmic expectations internalised as personal norms. This production of docility does not necessarily involve conscious manipulation or malicious intent on the part of platform designers. Rather, it emerges from the structural logic of systems designed to maximise engagement and extract value, systems that inevitably shape user behaviour in line with their operational imperatives, regardless of the therapeutic rhetoric surrounding them. As Capodivacca and Giacomini observe, "these technologies, while ostensibly therapeutic, can standardise and regulate grieving behaviours. This creates a form of 'programmed grief,' where personal mourning becomes shaped by algorithmic design" (Capodivacca & Giacomini, 2024, p. 227). The disciplinary power operating through grief technologies thus represents intensification and extension of earlier institutional controls over mourning, deploying unprecedented surveillance capabilities while presenting this as individualised support.

Biopolitics and the Management of Death

While disciplinary power primarily operates on individual bodies and behaviours, Foucault developed the concept of biopolitics to analyse power relations at the level of populations. Biopolitics concerns the techniques through which modern states and institutions manage populations as biological entities subject to calculation, optimisation, and intervention. Foucault explained this shift:

"One might say that the ancient right to take life or let live was replaced by a power to foster life or disallow it to the point of death" (Foucault, 1978, p. 138).

Where sovereign power claimed the right to take life or let live, biopower operates through the imperative to foster life or disallow it to the point of death. Biopower manages populations through statistical knowledge, public health interventions, regulations governing birth, death, disease, and reproduction, and all the mechanisms by which life itself becomes an object of political calculation and control. This shift from sovereignty to biopower represented a fundamental transformation in how power operates, from spectacular displays of the sovereign's right over death to subtle management of populations' vitality, health, and productivity.

Contemporary grief technologies extend biopower's operations into what might be termed thanatopolitics, the governance of death itself and the dead. Where traditional biopower focused on managing living populations' health, reproduction, and mortality rates, digital resurrection technologies claim authority beyond biological death, treating deceased persons' digital remains as resources requiring management, bereaved populations as subjects requiring regulation, and mourning itself as population-level behaviour amenable to algorithmic optimisation. Platforms accumulate statistical knowledge about grief patterns across demographic groups, deploy interventions designed to shape mourning trajectories, and constitute posthumous existence itself as a domain subject to corporate control. This represents biopower's ultimate expansion, extending governance from life through death into perpetual digital afterlives.

Grief technologies participate in the biopolitical management of death and mourning at the population scale. Platforms accumulate vast databases of mourning behaviour, generating statistical knowledge about how populations grieve, what temporal patterns characterise different types of loss, and what interventions appear to optimise adaptation. This knowledge enables what Capodivacca and Giacomini term "programmed grief," the algorithmic shaping of mourning according to norms derived from population-level data analysis (Capodivacca & Giacomini, 2024). The individual bereaved person becomes an element in the population of grievers whose aggregate behaviour can be measured, predicted, and optimised. Platform designers can test different interface features, compare outcomes across user segments, and identify patterns associated with prolonged engagement or successful grief resolution as defined by whatever metrics platforms choose to privilege. This biopolitical knowledge accumulation represents an extension of medical and psychiatric population-level grief research but operates at an unprecedented scale and with commercial rather than therapeutic objectives.

The management of death through biopolitical rationalities involves establishing norms for how populations should relate to mortality. Grief technologies participate in producing what might be termed "appropriate death," not in the medical sense of death occurring under desired circumstances, but rather in the biopolitical sense of death that is managed, regulated, and rendered productive for institutional interests. The dead become resources whose data can be harvested, whose simulations can generate ongoing revenue, whose continuing digital presence serves platform growth. The living bereaved, the 'grieving subject'*, become population segments to be analysed, categorised, and optimised, their mourning transformed from private suffering into data streams feeding algorithmic systems. This represents what Grandinetti et al (2020) describe as the emergence of haunted data and digital afterlives, where "data metrics 'bear traces of human, material, technical, symbolic, and imaginary histories' that function toward the systematic digital monitoring of people

---

* The 'grieving subject' can be understood not as a universal, essential human experience, but as a historically and culturally specific identity constituted by the power/knowledge

regimes that dictate how death and loss are perceived and managed in a given society.
or groups to regulate or govern behaviour" (Blackman, 2019, p. 166, cited in Grandinetti et al, 2020).

Foucault argued that biopower operates through what he termed "making live and letting die," the inversion of sovereign power's "taking life or letting live." Grief technologies instantiate this biopolitical logic by determining which forms of continuing bonds with the dead will be fostered and which will be disallowed. Platforms make decisions about what data persists, whose digital remains merit preservation, and what forms of posthumous presence receive technical and commercial support. These decisions reflect not neutral technological constraints but calculations about profitability, which, mourning practices, generate valuable data, and which populations represent attractive market segments. The result is biopolitical stratification whereby some deaths and some griefs receive technological support while others are left to die in the digital sense, denied the infrastructure for continued presence and connection.

The concept of necropolitics, developed by Mbembe to extend Foucault's biopolitics, provides additional analytical purchase on grief technologies. Mbembe argues that contemporary power creates "death-worlds," new and unique forms of social existence in which vast populations are subjected to conditions of life conferring upon them the status of living dead (Mbembe, 2003, p. 40). Grief technologies might be understood as creating particular forms of death-worlds in which the bereaved exist in states between connection and disconnection, between presence and absence, maintained in conditions that serve platform interests rather than supporting genuine adaptation to loss. The production of what might be termed "living death" or "digital zombification" occurs when platforms encourage indefinite continuation of mourning that generates ongoing revenue while potentially impeding the psychological work necessary for healthy adaptation.

Governmentality and the Conduct of Conduct

Foucault's concept of governmentality provides a framework for analysing how power operates not through direct coercion but through shaping the field of possible actions, through what he termed the "conduct of conduct." Governmentality concerns the ensemble of institutions, procedures, analyses, calculations, and tactics that allow the exercise of a specific, though complex, form of power having the population as its target, political economy as its major form of knowledge, and apparatuses of security as its essential technical instrument. Foucault defined government broadly as "the conduct of conduct: that is to say, a form of activity aiming to shape, guide or affect the conduct of some person or persons" (Foucault, cited in Capodivacca & Giacomini, 2024, p. 230). This represents a shift from earlier forms of power concerned primarily with territory or sovereignty to power concerned with managing populations through their own self-regulation, through techniques that lead individuals and groups to govern themselves according to particular rationalities and objectives.

Grief technologies operate within governmental rationalities that govern mourning through particular techniques and calculations. Platforms establish what Foucault would recognise as "regimes of practices," structured ways of doing things that shape how bereaved persons understand their options, make decisions, and conduct themselves. These regimes operate not through direct prohibition or compulsion but through the affordances platforms provide, the interactions they enable and constrain, the feedback they offer, and the temporal rhythms they establish. Users experience themselves as freely choosing to engage with grief technologies, yet these choices occur within parameters established by platform designs optimised for engagement and data extraction. This represents a sophisticated exercise of governmental power that operates through apparent freedom rather than overt control. As Bollmer observes, social media constitutes "part of a transformed governmentality, in which the 'nodal citizen' is expected to engage in and internalise proper conduct that includes connecting and maintaining flows while simultaneously managing the definitions and limits of their own life" (Bollmer, 2016, p. 7, 119).

The concept of "problematisation" provides an analytical tool for examining how governmentality functions. Problematisation refers to processes through which aspects of life become objects of thought, analysis, and intervention. Grief technologies participate in problematising mourning by constructing it as a condition requiring technological mediation, as a state that can and should be optimised through algorithmic intervention, as an experience inadequately supported by traditional communal or professional resources. This problematisation serves platform interests by creating markets for grief technologies, establishing rationales for continuous surveillance and data extraction, and positioning platforms as necessary intermediaries between bereaved and dead. The problematisation operates through medical and therapeutic discourses, suggesting that grief requires expert management, while commercial discourses emphasise technological innovation and individual choice.

Governmentality also involves what Foucault termed "technologies of the self," techniques through which individuals act upon themselves to achieve particular forms of subjectivity. Technologies of the self are practices that:

"permit individuals to effect by their own means or with the help of others a certain number of operations on their own bodies and souls, thoughts, conduct, and way of being, so as to transform themselves" (Foucault, 1988, p. 18).

Grief technologies function as technologies of the self by providing frameworks through which bereaved persons work upon their own grief, monitor their emotional states, evaluate their adaptation to loss, and attempt to optimise their mourning processes. Users internalise platform norms about appropriate grief, learn to recognise their own responses as healthy or pathological according to algorithmic standards, and undertake self-regulation aimed at achieving states defined by platforms as desirable outcomes. This represents governmental power at its most effective, when external control becomes internalised as self-discipline, when subjects actively participate in their own governance while experiencing this as autonomous self-care.

The rationalities governing grief technologies reflect what Foucault analysed as neoliberal governmentality, in which individuals become entrepreneurs of themselves, responsible for optimising their own human capital through calculated investments and strategic choices. Bereaved persons using grief technologies are positioned as consumers making rational decisions about which platforms to use, how frequently to engage, and which services to purchase, all while managing their grief as a form of emotional capital that requires investment and optimisation. This entrepreneurial subjectivity obscures how platform designs structure choices, how surveillance operates regardless of user awareness, and how commercial interests shape what appears as individual autonomy. The governmental rationality operating through grief technologies thus extends neoliberal logic into intimate domains of loss and mourning, rendering them markets for technological consumption and sites for the accumulation of valuable data.

Subjectivation and the Production of Grieving Subjects

Foucault's concept of subjectivation provides an essential framework for understanding how grief technologies do not simply act upon pre-existing subjects but rather participate in producing particular forms of grieving personhood. Subjectivation refers to processes through which individuals become subjects, through which they are constituted as particular kinds of persons with particular capacities, obligations, and ways of relating to themselves and others. This concept challenges humanist assumptions that treat the subject as foundational, autonomous, and pre-social. Instead, Foucault demonstrated that subjectivity is produced through power relations, through practices of division and classification, through techniques of examination and normalisation, through discourses that establish what counts as normal or pathological, healthy or sick, proper or deviant. As Foucault argued, the subject is not the source or origin of power relations but rather their effect, constituted through the very mechanisms that appear to act upon already-formed individuals.

Grief technologies participate in producing what might be termed the "technological grieving subject," a form of personhood characterised by particular relationships to loss, death, technology, and surveillance. This subject differs fundamentally from the communally grieving person of traditional societies or the therapeutically managed patient of medical institutions. The technological grieving subject experiences grief as requiring digital mediation, understands connection with the dead as achievable through algorithmic simulation, accepts comprehensive platform surveillance as a necessary condition for continued relationship, evaluates mourning success according to metrics embedded in interface designs, and disciplines personal emotional responses according to norms derived from population-level data analysis. This subject emerges not through conscious choice or deliberate self-fashioning but rather through the accumulated practices of platform engagement, through the habit formation that accompanies regular technological interaction, through the gradual normalisation of arrangements that might initially seem strange or problematic.

The production of technological grieving subjects operates through what Grandinetti et al. (2020), drawing on Wiley and Elam, term "synthetic subjectivation," a conceptual framework that challenges traditional distinctions between human and technological components of subjectivity. Wiley and Elam position synthetic subjectivation "as a way to conceptualise subject formation as grounded in compositions of heterogeneous elements, and not in humans or hominid organisms" (Wiley & Elam, 2018, p. 207). Despite different conceptualisations of how the subject is formed, subjectivation often functions to engineer "docile subjects as functional components of the sociotechnical megamachines of war, bureaucracy, and/or capital" (Wiley & Elam, 2018, p. 222). Applied to grief technologies, this perspective reveals how grieving subjectivity emerges from assemblages of human bodies, platform interfaces, algorithmic systems, data streams, server infrastructures, and representations of the dead. The bereaved person using griefbot cannot be understood as an autonomous individual who simply employs a technological tool. Rather, subjectivity itself becomes distributed across a human-technological assemblage in which boundaries between self and system, between mourner and platform, between living and dead become increasingly blurred and permeable.

What Grandinetti et al. (2020) describe as the "streaming subject" provides a model for understanding grief technology subjectivation. The streaming subject operates as an entanglement of machines, servers, data points, software, infrastructure, and algorithms rather than as a bounded corporeal entity. As Bollmer contends, "Social media produce the human as a 'posthuman' subject through a deeply ingrained and ultimately quotidian belief that it is in human nature to connect and circulate flows of information and capital," which "consequently reduces the subject of social media to data itself" (Bollmer, 2016, p. 133). Applied to grief, this suggests that the technological grieving subject extends beyond living human bodies to encompass what Blackman terms "haunted data," the digital traces of the deceased that continue circulating and generating effects long after biological death. The bereaved person engaging with griefbot becomes imbricated into a system in which their own data, the dead person's data, algorithmic processing systems, and platform infrastructures constitute a composite subjectivity that transcends individual human boundaries. Platforms know users better than users know themselves, as the common industry saying goes, not through supernatural insight but through comprehensive data accumulation and algorithmic analysis that renders subjects transparent to systems while systems remain opaque to subjects.

The production of data subjects represents a crucial dimension of technological subjectivation. Bereaved persons using grief technologies do not simply interact with platforms but rather become transformed into data profiles that can be analysed, compared, predicted, and optimised. Every interaction generates information streams that platforms capture and process, transforming lived emotional experiences into quantifiable metrics. The grief that was once understood as a profound existential disruption, as a social process requiring communal support, or as a psychological state requiring therapeutic intervention becomes a data pattern amenable to algorithmic management. This datafication of grief represents what Bollmer analyses as a reduction of social media subjects to data itself, where subjectivity becomes inseparable from the information traces subjects generate through platform engagement. The bereaved person exists simultaneously as a living human experiencing loss and as a data assemblage circulating through platform systems, with these dimensions increasingly indistinguishable in practice.

Foucault emphasised that subjectivation involves not only subjection to power but also the constitution of capacity for agency and resistance. Subjects are not simply passive effects of power but rather possess possibilities for contestation and transformation precisely because they are products of power relations rather than natural givens. Where there is power, Foucault argued, there is resistance, "not as the opposite of power but as its permanent condition and consequence" (Foucault, 1978). Applied to grief technologies, this suggests that while platforms produce particular forms of technological grieving subjectivity, these productions remain incomplete, contested, and open to refusal. Users develop tactical resistances to platform demands, finding ways to subvert surveillance, to use systems against their intended purposes, to maintain forms of mourning that exceed algorithmic parameters. The technological grieving subject is not simply a docile consumer but rather a site of ongoing struggle between platform imperatives and user autonomy, between algorithmic governance and human resistance, between commercial exploitation and genuine support for bereavement.

Archaeological and Genealogical Methods

Foucault developed two complementary methodological approaches for analysing how knowledge and power relations operate: archaeology and genealogy. These methods provide practical analytical tools for examining grief technologies rather than simply theoretical frameworks. Archaeology concerns itself with discourses, with the systems of statements, concepts, and practices that establish what counts as knowledge in particular historical periods. Archaeological analysis examines the rules governing what can be said, who is authorised to speak, what counts as evidence or truth, and what objects and subjects discourse produces. In *The Archaeology of Knowledge*, Foucault defined discourse as "practices that systematically form the objects of which they speak" (Foucault, 1969, p. 54). Genealogy, as discussed in Chapter Two, traces how present arrangements emerged through historical contingency, through struggles and contestations, through exercises of power rather than discoveries of truth. Genealogical analysis reveals discontinuities, ruptures, and transformations rather than assuming smooth evolution or progressive enlightenment.

Archaeological method applied to grief technologies examines the discursive formations through which these systems are understood, legitimised, and deployed. This involves analysing the ensemble of statements made about grief technologies by platform designers, marketing materials, media coverage, academic research, regulatory discussions, and user testimonials. Archaeological analysis reveals the implicit rules governing these discourses, the assumptions they share, the authorities they recognise, the evidence they privilege, and the alternatives they exclude. For instance, grief technology discourse typically positions platforms as providing support for natural psychological processes, as enabling healthy continuing bonds, and as offering innovative solutions to universal human needs. This discourse obscures power relations, commercial interests, surveillance mechanisms, and alternatives to technological mediation. Archaeological analysis makes visible these obscured dimensions by examining what discourse makes thinkable and unthinkable, sayable and unsayable, legitimate and illegitimate.

The concept of episteme, Foucault's term for the underlying structure of knowledge characteristic of a particular historical period, provides an analytical tool for understanding how grief technologies operate within broader contemporary rationalities.

"By *episteme* we mean, in fact, the total set of relations that
        unite, at a given period, the discursive practices that give
            rise to epistemological figures, sciences, and possibly

formalized systems; the way in which, in each of these discursive formations, the transitions to epistemologization, scientificity, and formalization are situated and operate; the distribution of these thresholds, which may coincide, be subordinated to one another, or be separated by shifts in time; the lateral relations that may exist between epistemological figures or sciences in so far as they belong to neighbouring, but distinct, discursive practices. The episteme is [. . .] the totality of relations that can be discovered, for a given period, between the sciences when one analyses them at the level of discursive regularities." (Foucault, 1969, p.191).

The current episteme, characterised by what might be termed "digital solutionism" or "technological determinism," assumes that human problems require technological solutions, that innovation represents progress, and that digital mediation enables rather than constrains human connection. Grief technologies make sense within this episteme, appearing as natural applications of available technological capabilities to address universal human experiences. Archaeological analysis denaturalises this by revealing how different epistemes would render grief technologies strange or problematic, how alternative rationalities might approach loss and mourning differently, and how current arrangements reflect particular historical configurations of knowledge and power rather than universal truths.

Genealogical method, as demonstrated in Chapter Two's historical analysis, traces how current grief technology arrangements emerged through contingent historical processes. This involves examining not simply linear development but rather discontinuities, struggles, and power relations that shaped contemporary configurations. Foucault explained

Genealogy is a form of critical history in the sense that it attempts a diagnosis of 'the present time, and of what we are, in this very moment' in order 'to question ... what is postulated as self-evident ... to dissipate what is familiar and accepted' (Foucault 1988a, p.265).

Genealogy reveals that technological governance of grief was not an inevitable consequence of innovation but rather an outcome of particular institutional interests, commercial opportunities, regulatory failures, and cultural transformations. The genealogical approach enables critical distance from contemporary arrangements by showing they could have been and could yet be otherwise, that alternatives existed and continue to exist, that current configurations serve particular interests while presenting themselves as serving universal needs.

Applied to specific grief technologies, genealogical analysis examines how particular platforms emerged, what interests they served, what alternatives they displaced, what resistances they encountered, and how they transformed in response to contestation. For instance, the history of social media memorialisation reveals struggles over who controls posthumous data, conflicts between platform interests in data retention and user desires for deletion, tensions between commercial imperatives and ethical responsibilities, and transformations in interface designs responding to user complaints while maintaining surveillance capabilities. This genealogical understanding reveals grief technologies as products of ongoing struggles rather than as static solutions to fixed problems, opening possibilities for continued contestation and transformation.

Analytical Tools for Critical Analysis

The Foucauldian concepts elaborated in this chapter (disciplinary power, biopolitics, governmentality, subjectivation, archaeology, and genealogy) do not operate in isolation but rather function as an integrated analytical framework for examining grief technologies. This framework enables systematic analysis of how power operates through technological systems that appear to serve individual needs while actually serving institutional interests, how subjects are produced through practices that appear to support autonomy while actually constraining it, and how commercial exploitation presents itself as therapeutic intervention. The integration of these concepts provides a comprehensive critical apparatus for understanding grief technologies as complex assemblages through which mourning is governed, commodified, and rendered productive for platform capitalism.

Disciplinary power and biopolitics work together to analyse how grief technologies operate simultaneously at individual and population levels. Platforms   discipline   individual   users   through   surveillance   and normalisation while accumulating population-level knowledge that enables aggregate management of mourning behaviours. Governmentality connects these dimensions by examining how individuals are led to govern themselves according to norms that serve platform interests, how apparent freedom and choice occur within parameters established by commercial imperatives. Subjectivation reveals how these power relations produce particular forms of grieving personhood rather than simply acting upon pre-existing subjects. Archaeological and genealogical methods provide techniques for examining the discourses legitimating these arrangements and the historical processes through which they emerged.

This integrated framework enables analysis that moves beyond surface features of grief technologies to examine their operation as mechanisms of power and control. Rather than accepting platform claims about therapeutic support at face value, Foucauldian analysis reveals how these technologies function as apparatuses through which mourning is surveilled, disciplined, commodified, and rendered governable. Rather than treating technological mediation of grief as neutral innovation, critical analysis examines whose interests are served, what alternatives are foreclosed, and what forms of resistance remain possible. Rather than assuming that current arrangements represent the inevitable consequences of technological progress, a genealogical perspective reveals the contingent character of contemporary configurations and the possibilities for alternative futures.

The subsequent chapters of this book apply this Foucauldian framework to specific dimensions of grief technologies. Chapter Four examines surveillance capitalism and the commodification of grief, analysing how platforms extract value from emotional labour and transform mourning into a profitable commodity. Chapter Five explores algorithmic governmentality, examining how interface designs discipline mourning behaviours and produce programmed grief. Chapter Six investigates subjectivation in detail, analysing the production of data subjects and the transformation of grieving personhood through technological mediation. Each of these analyses draws on the conceptual tools developed in this chapter, demonstrating their practical utility for critical examination of how grief technologies operate as exercises of power rather than neutral supports for bereavement.

Understanding grief technologies through a Foucauldian framework matters not simply for academic analysis but for practical intervention and resistance. Recognising these systems as apparatuses of power rather than therapeutic tools enables bereaved persons to make more informed decisions about whether and how to engage with them. Identifying mechanisms of surveillance and normalisation enables the development of tactics to subvert platform control and maintain autonomous mourning practices. Revealing commercial interests obscured by therapeutic rhetoric enables political organising around regulation, alternatives, and collective resistance. The Foucauldian framework thus provides not only analytical tools but also resources for contestation, for imagining and creating different arrangements in which societies might support bereaved persons without subjecting them to comprehensive surveillance or commercial exploitation. The critical analysis enabled by these concepts serves the ultimate purpose of expanding possibilities for mourning that are genuinely supportive rather than systematically exploitative, that respect grief's complexity rather than reducing it to optimisable behaviour, and that preserve space for resistance rather than producing only docility and compliance.

References

Blackman, L. (2019). *Haunted data: Affect, transmedia, weird science.* Bloomsbury Academic.

Bollmer, G. (2016). *Inhuman networks: Social media and the archaeology of connection.* Bloomsbury Academic.

Capodivacca, S., & Giacomini, G. (2024). Discipline and power in the digital age: Critical reflections from Foucault's thought. *Foucault Studies*, 36(1), 227–251. https://doi.org/10.22439/fs.i36.7215

Foucault, M. (1969). Michael Foucault, Archaeology of Knowledge. *Translated by AM Sheridan Smith. London and New York: Routledge.*

Foucault, M. (1975). *Discipline and punish: The birth of the prison.* (A. Sheridan, Trans.). Vintage Books.

Foucault, M. (1977). *Discipline and Punish: The Birth of the Prison.* Trans. A. Sheridan. London: Allen Lane.

Foucault, M. (1978). *The history of sexuality, Volume 1: An introduction.* (R. Hurley, Trans.). Pantheon Books.

Foucault, M. (1980). *Power/knowledge: Selected interviews and other writings, 1972-1977.* (C. Gordon, Ed.). Pantheon Books.

Foucault, M. (1988). *Technologies of the self.* In L. H. Martin, H. Gutman, & P. H. Hutton (Eds.), *Technologies of the self: A seminar with Michel Foucault* (pp. 16–49). University of Massachusetts Press.

Grandinetti, J., DeAtley, T., & Bruinsma, J. (2020). THE DEAD SPEAK: BIG DATA AND DIGITALLY MEDIATED DEATH. *AoIR Selected Papers of Internet Research, 2020.* https://doi.org/10.5210/spir.v2020i0.11122

Mbembe, A. (2003). Necropolitics. *Public Culture*, 15(1), 11–40.

Wiley, S., & Elam, J. (2018). Synthetic subjectivation: Technical media and the composition of posthuman subjects. *Subjectivity*, 11(3), 203–227.

FOUR

Surveillance Capitalism and the Commodification of Grief

The Foucauldian framework developed in Chapter Three provides analytical tools for examining how grief technologies operate as mechanisms of power, disciplining mourning behaviours and producing particular forms of grieving subjects. But understanding these power relations fully requires examining the economic structures within which grief technologies function, the material interests they serve, and the processes through which intimate experiences of loss become transformed into sources of profit. This chapter analyses grief technologies through the lens of surveillance capitalism and critical political economy, revealing how mourning has been enclosed within commercial platforms, how bereaved persons' emotional labour generates extractable value, and how the dead themselves become resources whose data can be indefinitely exploited. The transformation of grief from communal social practice or private psychological experience into profitable commodity represents not neutral technological innovation but rather what Andrejevic terms "digital enclosure," the appropriation of previously non-commodified domains of human activity into circuits of capital accumulation (Andrejevic, 2007, p. 296).

Understanding this economic dimension matters because it reveals whose interests grief technologies actually serve. Platform companies present their services through therapeutic rhetoric emphasising support, connection, and healing, obscuring the commercial imperatives driving their development and operation. Examining the business models, revenue structures, and data extraction practices underlying grief technologies exposes how platforms profit from vulnerability, how they design systems to maximise engagement rather than support healthy mourning, and how they treat bereaved persons primarily as sources of valuable data rather than as individuals requiring genuine care. This critical economic analysis complements the Foucauldian examination of power relations by revealing the material foundations upon which those relations rest, the profit motives that shape how disciplinary mechanisms operate, and the commodification processes that transform subjects into data and grief into extractable resources.

Digital Enclosure and the Commodification of Grieving

The concept of digital enclosure provides a framework for understanding how grief technologies appropriate mourning into commercial platforms. Andrejevic uses this term to describe how online platforms capture user activity that was previously performed outside commercial spaces, transforming it into data that the platforms own and control. Digital enclosure operates through "an increasingly detailed and fine-grained" ability "to capture and store patterns of interaction, movement, transaction, and communication" (Andrejevic, 2007, p. 296). Applied to grief, this means that mourning practices that once occurred through face-to-face communal rituals, private remembrance, or therapeutic relationships are now mediated through technological platforms that surveil every interaction, capture comprehensive data on emotional responses, and retain ownership of the information generated by these intimate experiences.

The enclosure of mourning within digital platforms represents a transformation in both the spatial and economic organisation of grief. Spatially, mourning moves from physical locations (cemeteries, homes, places of worship, therapists' offices) into virtual environments controlled by technology companies. This spatial shift enables unprecedented surveillance, as platforms can monitor interactions impossible to observe in physical spaces, can collect data at scales and granularities unachievable through human observation, and can persist indefinitely while physical gatherings are necessarily temporary. Economically, grief moves from domains governed by kinship obligations, professional ethics, or communal reciprocity into the commercial marketplace where platform interests in profit maximisation shape how mourning is structured, what forms of expression are enabled or constrained, and how long engagement continues.

Grandinetti et al (2020) observe that "the expansion of cultural practices like mourning onto social media platforms are enclosed, surveilled, and then modified in such a way that aligns with the economic interests of the platform" (Grandinetti et al, 2020). This modification occurs through interface designs that encourage particular types of engagement, through algorithmic systems that determine what content appears and when, through notification mechanisms that prompt continued interaction, and through temporal structures that establish rhythms of platform use. Users experience themselves as freely choosing to engage with platforms for mourning, yet these choices occur within parameters established to serve commercial rather than therapeutic objectives. The enclosure is effective precisely because it appears voluntary, because platforms present themselves as providing valuable services rather than appropriating previously non-commodified practices.

The privatisation accompanying digital enclosure transforms grief from a collective social process into an individualised platform-mediated experience. Traditional mourning practices, for all their problems and restrictions, embedded loss within networks of mutual obligation and communal support. Funerals brought extended families and communities together, memorial practices involved collective participation, and ongoing remembrance occurred through shared rituals and reciprocal care. Digital enclosure fragments these collective dimensions, isolating bereaved persons in private interactions with screens. As Jiménez-Alonso and Brescó de Luna note, while "co-presence between mourners and loved ones is socially shared within the same virtual space" on social networking sites, with griefbots, this co-presence is confined to the private conversational space between the mourner and the deceased person. This privatisation serves platform interests by eliminating communal oversight that might constrain commercial exploitation, by individualising what was collective, thereby expanding market segments, and by fragmenting potential collective resistance to platform power.

The concept of enclosure originally described how common lands in early modern Europe were appropriated by private owners, transforming resources that communities shared into property controlled by individuals or corporations for profit. Digital enclosure operates through a similar logic, appropriating practices and experiences previously outside market relations into commercial platforms. Grief technologies enclose not physical lands but rather emotional territories, transforming mourning from an activity governed by social norms, professional ethics, or personal autonomy into a commercial transaction governed by terms of service, platform policies, and profit imperatives. The bereaved person using grief technology may experience this as gaining access to innovative services, but from a critical economic perspective, they are being enclosed within systems designed to extract value from their vulnerability while presenting this extraction as support.

The Microsoft patent, noted in Chapter 1, makes explicit what other platforms obscure: grief data becomes a proprietary corporate asset through technical processing. The patent describes creating 'a special index in the theme of the specific person's personality' from social data, including images, voice recordings, messages, and behavioural information (Abramson & Johnson, 2020). This 'personality index' functions as intellectual property owned by the platform rather than the deceased person or their survivors. The patent further specifies that voice fonts and three-dimensional models can be generated from data of deceased persons, revealing how platforms envision monetising grief through sellable products (Abramson & Johnson, 2020). The technical architecture described in the patent demonstrates that commercial extraction is not incidental to grief technologies but rather their designed purpose.

Free Labour and Affective Capitalism

The extraction of value from grief technologies operates partly through what Terranova terms "free labour," the unpaid work users perform while engaging with digital platforms. Terranova argues that cultural and technical labour produced in digital spaces is "not developed simply as an answer to the economic needs of capital" but rather "in relation to the expansion of the cultural industries and they are part of a process of economic experimentation with the creation of monetary value out of knowledge / culture / affect" (Terranova, 2004, p. 79). Applied to grief technologies, this means that bereaved persons' interactions with platforms, the emotional expressions they share, and the data they generate through mourning practices all constitute labour that creates value for platforms while users receive no compensation.

Every message sent to a griefbot, every visit to a memorial page, every minute spent in virtual reality memorial space represents work that generates valuable data. This work is experienced by users not as labour but as personal mourning, as private emotional expression, as voluntary engagement with services they find meaningful. Yet from a platform perspective, user activity constitutes productive labour that creates information assets platforms own and can monetise through multiple revenue streams. The labour is free in a double sense: users perform it without payment, and they typically do so without recognising it as labour, experiencing platform engagement as an autonomous activity rather than as unpaid work generating profit for corporations.

The affective dimension of this labour requires particular attention. Grief technologies do not simply extract data about actions but rather about emotions, about intimate psychological states, about vulnerability and suffering. This represents what scholars term "affective capitalism," economic systems that appropriate human feelings and emotions as resources for value creation. Bereaved persons using grief technologies expose their deepest sorrows, their ongoing struggles with loss, and their most private thoughts about the deceased, all of which become data that platforms capture, analyse, and utilise. The commercialisation of affect in this context raises profound ethical questions, as platforms profit from emotional states characterised by vulnerability, as they design systems to intensify rather than resolve grief if doing so increases engagement, as they treat human suffering primarily as an opportunity for value extraction.

Grandinetti et al. (2020) note that "everything we do on a social media platform, from liking to posting to updating our privacy settings, is a potential commodity" (Grandinetti et al, 2020). This commodification of activity extends to mourning, transforming expressions of grief into data products. The bereaved person clicking on the memorial notification, responding to the algorithm's suggestion to interact with a representation of the dead, and sharing memories through the platform's interface all generate information that platforms package and sell. Users may derive genuine comfort from these activities, but this does not negate the economic exploitation occurring simultaneously. The dual character of platform engagement, experienced by users as meaningful while serving as unpaid labour that generates profit, is a characteristic feature of digital capitalism that grief technologies exemplify with particular clarity, given the vulnerability of their user base.

The concept of free labour reveals how platforms externalise costs while privatising profits. Traditional therapeutic support for grief requires paid professionals, ongoing institutional resources, and physical spaces for meetings. Grief technologies shift much of this labour onto bereaved persons themselves, who perform the emotional work of mourning through platform interfaces while platforms capture value generated through this unpaid activity. Users may experience reduced costs compared to professional therapy, but the economic benefit accrues primarily to platforms that avoid paying for the labour they appropriate. This externalisation of costs while capturing value produced represents a fundamental mechanism of platform capitalism that grief technologies deploy in a domain characterised by particular vulnerability and need.

The Cyberproletariat and the Labour of the Dead

The extraction of value from grief technologies operates not only through the free labour of living users but also through what might be termed the perpetual labour of the dead themselves. The data of deceased persons continues generating value for platforms long after biological life ends, creating what Dyer-Witheford terms the "cyberproletariat," the "planetary working class tasked with working itself out of a job, toiling relentlessly to develop a system of robots and networks, networked robots and robot networks, for which the human is ultimately surplus to requirements" (Dyer-Witheford, 2015, p. 15). Applied to grief technologies, this suggests that the dead become permanent members of the digital labour force, their data continuously exploited to generate engagement and revenue without the possibility of withdrawal or compensation.

Öhman and Watson project that there will be over 1.4 billion Facebook profiles of deceased users by the year 2100, "leading to questions of the dead overtaking the living online" (Öhman & Watson, 2019, cited in Grandinetti et al., 2020). This massive accumulation of dead users' data represents an enormous resource for platforms. The information persists indefinitely on servers, can be analysed and reanalysed, can generate ongoing interactions with living users who visit memorial pages or engage with AI simulations of the deceased, and can be incorporated into algorithmic systems that learn from patterns across millions of dead users' historical behaviours. As Grandinetti et al.(2020) observe, "data decay and loss are concerns that can affect the circulation of user data, but many platforms have various backups that can restore data much beyond the average lifespan of a user" (Grandinetti et al., 2020, citing Cheng, 2006; Miller, 2015).

The perpetual labour of the dead raises questions about exploitation that extend beyond traditional labour relations. Living workers can withdraw their labour, can organise collectively to demand better conditions, and can negotiate terms of employment. The dead possess no such capacities. Their data continues to generate value for platforms, regardless of what they might have wanted, regardless of whether their families consent, regardless of any ethical considerations about posthumous dignity or autonomy. Platforms own and control this data according to terms of service agreed during life, but extending indefinitely after death, creating what might be termed "digital serfdom" in which the dead remain permanently bound to platforms that profit from their ongoing exploitation.

The economic value of dead users' data derives from multiple sources. Memorial pages generate ongoing visits from bereaved persons, creating opportunities for targeted advertising based on comprehensive information about visitors' emotional states and relationships. Historical data from dead users contributes to algorithmic training, improving systems' ability to predict and influence the behaviours of living users. The sheer volume of data from deceased users creates network effects that increase platform value, as more comprehensive databases enable more sophisticated analysis and more effective engagement optimisation. Grandinetti et al. (2020) note that "the data contribution from dead user accounts is not insubstantial when compared to live users and is a specific, targetable point from which platforms can profit" (Grandinetti et al. 2020).

The transformation of dead users into a permanent digital labour force represents an extension of capitalist logic beyond traditional boundaries. Where classical capitalism extracted surplus value from living workers' labour, surveillance capitalism extracts value from data that transcends life and death. The cyberproletariat includes not only living workers but also the dead, whose information continues circulating and generating profit indefinitely. This represents what Grandinetti et al. (2020) describe: "when the dead are made to provide perpetual free labour, then the networked subject becomes a continuous member" of the cyberproletariat (Grandinetti et al., 2020). The development of grief technologies intensifies this exploitation by creating new forms of engagement with dead users' data, new revenue streams from mourning, and new mechanisms for extracting value from death itself.

Platform Business Models and Revenue Structures

Understanding how grief technologies extract value requires examining their specific business models and revenue structures. Platforms generate income through multiple mechanisms, each with implications for how mourning is shaped, what behaviours are encouraged, and what interests are served. The predominant models include subscription services, freemium arrangements, advertising revenue, and data sales, often deployed in combination to maximise extraction while maintaining the appearance of user benefit.

Subscription models require users to pay recurring fees for access to grief technology services. As described in research on speculative grief technology products, services like "Paren't" and "Stay" charge bereaved persons monthly subscriptions to maintain access to AI simulations of the deceased (Hollanek & Nowaczyk-Basińska, 2024). This creates a perverse incentive structure in which platforms profit from extended rather than resolved grief. If mourning proceeds healthily toward adaptation and acceptance, users may reduce or cease platform engagement, eliminating subscription revenue. Platforms, therefore, have a financial interest in encouraging prolonged dependence, in designing systems that foster an ongoing need for simulations, and in creating conditions where bereaved persons feel unable to discontinue service without experiencing what they perceive as a second loss of the deceased.

The freemium model, deployed by platforms like Replika, offers basic services without charge while requiring payment for enhanced features. As Fabry and Alfano observe,

"many of the prominent players in this space, such as Replika, use a freemium subscription model. Basic accounts are free, but the more engaging ones require" payment (Fabry & Alfano, 2024, p. 766).

This structure creates multiple problems. First, it establishes grief as a gateway to upselling, with platforms using basic services to establish emotional dependencies that can then be exploited through premium offerings. Second, it creates stratified access to mourning support based on ability to pay, with wealthier bereaved persons receiving more sophisticated simulations while poorer users must accept inferior alternatives. Third, it incentivises designing free tiers to be deliberately unsatisfying, ensuring users feel compelled to upgrade while platforms maintain the appearance of providing accessible support.

Advertising constitutes a major revenue source for grief technologies embedded within larger social media platforms. Grandinetti et al. (2020) explain that "social media platforms rely on advertising to fund their production and growth, and advertising in digital environments is tied near exclusively to algorithmic engagement" (Grandinetti et al., 2020). Memorial pages, grief-related content, and mourning activities generate valuable advertising opportunities precisely because bereaved persons' emotional vulnerability makes them particularly susceptible to targeted marketing. Platforms know users are experiencing loss, can infer details about relationships and circumstances of death, and can identify moments of heightened emotional need. This information enables extraordinarily precise targeting of products and services to vulnerable populations, transforming grief into a profitable marketing opportunity while presenting platforms as providing supportive spaces for mourning.

Data sales or licensing represent perhaps the most troubling revenue mechanism, as platforms package and sell information about bereaved persons' mourning behaviours, emotional states, and relationships. While platforms typically claim they anonymise such data, the granularity and volume of information collected through grief technologies make true anonymisation difficult, if not impossible. As discussed in legal scholarship on digital resurrection, "capturing personal data empowers predictive purchasing algorithms" and enables numerous commercial applications (discussed in Puzio, 2025). The bereaved person using grief technology may not realise that their intimate expressions of sorrow, their conversations with AI simulations of the dead, and their patterns of memorial page visits all become commodities sold to data brokers, advertisers, researchers, and potentially other commercial interests.

These business models share a common feature: they treat grief primarily as an opportunity for value extraction rather than as a human experience requiring genuine support. Platform designs reflect economic imperatives rather than therapeutic principles. Interface features that maximise engagement take precedence over those that might support healthy mourning. Notification systems prioritise continued platform use over user well-being. Algorithmic recommendations aim to increase time spent on platforms, regardless of whether such engagement serves the interests of bereaved persons. The fundamental misalignment between commercial objectives and therapeutic needs means that even well-intentioned platform features operate within economic structures that systematically prioritise profit over user benefit.

The Political Economy of Death in the Age of Information

The commodification of grief through technological platforms represents what Öhman and Floridi term "the political economy of death in the age of information," a systematic transformation of mortality and mourning into domains governed by economic calculation and commercial exploitation (Öhman & Floridi, 2017). This political economy operates through multiple interconnected processes: the enclosure of mourning within commercial platforms, the extraction of value through free labour, the perpetual exploitation of dead users' data, and the deployment of business models that prioritise profit over user wellbeing. Together, these processes constitute a regime of accumulation in which death itself becomes a resource, grief becomes a market, and bereaved persons become simultaneously consumers and unpaid workers generating value for corporations.

Understanding this political economy requires recognising that grief technologies do not exist in isolation but rather participate in broader systems of surveillance capitalism. Zuboff defines surveillance capitalism as an economic system predicated on:

> "unilateral claiming of private human experience as free raw material for translation into behavioural data", which are then "computed and packaged as prediction products and sold into *behavioural futures markets*" (Zuboff, 2019, p. 8, emphasis original).

Grief technologies exemplify this logic with particular clarity. Mourning constitutes a deeply private human experience that platforms claim as raw material, transforming intimate emotional states into behavioural data. This data enables the prediction of bereaved persons' future actions, emotional trajectories, and commercial susceptibilities, information that has substantial value in futures markets that trade on the ability to anticipate and influence behaviour.

While platforms publicly frame grief technologies as services that support bereaved individuals, technical documentation reveals the commercial imperatives that drive development. Patent filings, unlike marketing materials, specify actual mechanisms through which platforms envision extracting value from death. The Microsoft patent's technical specifications make explicit the commercial logic that other platforms obscure through euphemistic language about connection and remembrance. The patent describes a systematic transformation process through which deceased persons become corporate assets, generating multiple revenue streams. This transformation occurs through three distinct stages, each of which converts aspects of human identity into proprietary products.

First, the patent describes extracting data from deceased persons to create corporate intellectual property. The technical specifications state that "the social data may be used to create or modify a special index in the theme of the specific person's personality" (Abramson & Johnson, 2020). This "special index" functions not as a neutral representation but rather as a proprietary asset owned by the platform. The deceased person's communications, photographs, behavioural patterns, and social media activity become raw materials that platforms process into personality indices they control. The transformation from human being to "special index" represents the foundational commodification upon which subsequent profit extraction depends.

Second, the patent describes generating sellable vocal products from recordings of deceased persons. The specifications explain that

> "a voice font of the specific person may be generated using recordings and sound data related to the specific person" (Abramson & Johnson, 2020).

Voice fonts constitute commercial products that platforms can license, sell, or deploy across multiple services. The deceased person's distinctive vocal characteristics, extracted from personal recordings never intended for commercial use, become assets that the platform owns and monetises. What bereaved family members experience as hearing their loved one's voice again constitutes, from the platform's perspective, the deployment of proprietary voice synthesis technology that generates revenue through continued user engagement.

Third, the patent describes creating three-dimensional visual models as commercial products. The technical architecture specifies that

"a 2D or 3D model of a specific person may be generated using images, depth information, and/or video data associated with the specific person" (Abramson & Johnson, 2020).

These models function as sellable products that can be deployed across virtual, augmented, and gaming platforms. The deceased person's physical appearance, reconstructed from photographs and videos, becomes a visual asset owned by the platform. Family photographs shared in private contexts become source material for commercial three-dimensional models that platforms control and monetise.

This three-stage transformation reveals grief technologies' underlying business model: extract data from deceased persons, process it into proprietary indices and products, then monetise those products through ongoing engagement with bereaved users. The patent makes no distinction between deceased persons whose families consent to such processing and those whose data is extracted without their families' consent. The technical specifications treat all deceased persons' data as an available resource for corporate transformation into "special indices," voice fonts, and 3D models. Once platforms have access to a deceased person's social data, they can convert human identity into intellectual property that generates revenue through multiple product deployments. This transformation chain, documented in the Microsoft patent, represents not an aberration but rather a blueprint for the grief technology industry. The technical specifications reveal what platform marketing obscures: deceased persons function as raw materials for profit extraction, bereaved users as ongoing revenue sources, and grief itself as a business opportunity.

The public disclosure of Microsoft patents, mandated by the patent system's requirement for technical specificity in exchange for monopoly rights, provides permanent documented evidence of how major technology corporations conceptualise grief technologies. Unlike marketing materials that emphasise connection and remembrance, the patent's legal language reveals the actual commercial architecture: deceased persons transformed into 'special indices' that generate 'voice fonts' and '3D models' as sellable products. Microsoft's subsequent public disavowal of its implementation intentions, following negative media coverage, demonstrates the gap between corporate strategy documented in legal filings and public relations messaging deployed for reputation management

The concentration of power within platform companies, despite the growing diversity of grief technology providers, intensifies the exploitative character of this political economy. Grief technologies operate through platforms controlled by major technology corporations, venture capital-backed startups offering griefbots and digital resurrection services, and an expanding array of smaller developers entering the market. Yet this proliferation of providers has not fundamentally altered asymmetric power relations in which platforms set the terms of service, govern data use, and determine what constitutes acceptable mourning behaviour, all without meaningful input from bereaved users or democratic oversight. Users possess little bargaining power, as switching costs remain high (losing access to accumulated memorial content or established AI simulations) and genuine alternatives are limited. The result is what might be termed "digital feudalism," in which platforms exercise lordship over territories of grief, while bereaved persons occupy a position analogous to that of serfs, bound to platforms that appropriate value from their labour while providing minimal reciprocal obligations.

The transformation of grief into a commodity raises questions about domains that should remain outside market relations. Not all human experiences can or should be subject to commercial exploitation. Certain practices, relationships, and emotional states might possess intrinsic value that is degraded or destroyed when they become primarily economic transactions. The commodification of mourning threatens to reduce profound existential experience to optimisable behaviour, to transform relationships with the dead into a product to be consumed, to subordinate genuine emotional processes to commercial imperatives. As discussed in legal scholarship examining the commodification of digital remains, "the question is whether personal data of the deceased, an asset without an inherent value, should be recognised as possessing a value that is not monetary" (Puzio, 2025, p. 1605) and whether moral personhood concerns should constrain commercial exploitation.

The political economy of death in the information age also involves what Marx termed 'primitive accumulation,' the violent appropriation of resources that establishes the conditions for capitalist production. Applied to grief technologies, primitive accumulation occurs through platforms' initial claiming of mourning as a domain for commercial exploitation, their appropriation of data previously outside market relations, and their enclosure of practices formerly governed by communal norms or professional ethics. This appropriation was not an inevitable consequence of technological development but rather a deliberate strategy pursued by corporations that identified vulnerable populations as potential market segments. The transformation of grief into a profitable commodity required active effort to enclose, surveil, and commercialise experiences previously protected from such exploitation, an effort that continues through platform policies designed to expand and intensify the extraction of value from mourning.

Resistance to Commodification and Alternative Economies

Understanding grief technologies through the framework of surveillance capitalism and political economy reveals not only how they exploit mourning but also where possibilities for resistance emerge. The commodification of grief is neither complete nor irreversible. Bereaved persons resist platform demands through tactical refusals, the development of alternative practices, and collective organising around regulation and democratic control. Analysing these resistances matters because they point toward possibilities for different arrangements, for ways of supporting mourning that do not require subjecting bereaved persons to comprehensive surveillance and commercial exploitation.

Individual resistance takes multiple forms. Some bereaved persons refuse to engage with grief technologies altogether, maintaining mourning practices outside commercial platforms despite social pressures and technological affordances encouraging digital engagement. Others use platforms tactically, extracting value they find meaningful while resisting demands for comprehensive data disclosure or extended engagement. Still others employ technical means to subvert surveillance, using privacy tools to limit data collection, creating deliberately misleading information to poison algorithmic profiles, and withdrawing from platforms once immediate needs are satisfied rather than becoming long-term subscribers. These individual resistances may not transform systemic power relations, but they demonstrate that platform control is never total, that users maintain capacities for refusal and subversion even within asymmetric power structures.

Collective resistance operates at a larger scale through organising around regulation, through demanding democratic oversight of platform practices, and through creating alternative technological arrangements governed by principles other than profit maximisation. Various advocacy organisations push for stronger data protection laws, for requirements that platforms obtain meaningful consent before commodifying grief, and for restrictions on how information about deceased persons can be exploited. The European Union's General Data Protection Regulation and proposed AI Act represent attempts to constrain commercial exploitation of personal data, including information generated through mourning. While these regulations face limitations and platforms often find ways to circumvent them, they establish the principle that commodification of grief cannot proceed without constraints, that democratic societies possess legitimate authority to regulate how corporations profit from human vulnerability.

Alternative technological arrangements point toward possibilities beyond surveillance capitalism. Commons-based approaches to grief technology might enable digital support for mourning without subjecting bereaved persons to commercial exploitation. Cooperatively owned platforms governed by users rather than shareholders, open-source software enabling grief support without proprietary control, publicly funded services operating according to therapeutic rather than profit objectives, all represent alternatives to the dominant commercial model. While such alternatives face significant challenges given platforms' concentrated power and resources, their existence demonstrates that current arrangements are not inevitable, that grief technologies could be organised according to different principles serving different interests.

The transformation of mourning from a commodity back into a communal practice, or into a domain governed by genuine therapeutic principles rather than profit motives, requires not simply individual resistance or alternative technologies, but rather broader political struggle over how societies organise support for bereaved persons. This struggle involves challenging the enclosure of grief within commercial platforms, demanding democratic control over technological systems that mediate fundamental human experiences, and insisting that certain domains must remain outside market relations regardless of the profit opportunities they present. The critical analysis of surveillance capitalism and political economy developed in this chapter provides conceptual resources for such struggles by revealing the material interests underlying grief technologies, by exposing the exploitation obscured by therapeutic rhetoric, and by demonstrating how platforms profit from vulnerability while claiming to provide support.

Understanding grief technologies as mechanisms of surveillance capitalism rather than as neutral innovations transforms how we evaluate them. Rather than asking whether they provide effective therapeutic support (they may or may not), critical political economy asks whose interests they serve, how they extract value from mourning, and what alternatives they foreclose. Rather than accepting platform claims about user benefit at face value, economic analysis examines business models, revenue structures, and data practices that reveal commercial imperatives driving development and operation. Rather than treating the commodification of grief as an inevitable consequence of technological progress, the historical materialist perspective recognises it as an outcome of specific political-economic arrangements that can be contested and transformed. The subsequent chapters continue examining specific mechanisms through which grief technologies operate as exercises of power, always within the context of the economic structures revealed by this critical analysis of surveillance capitalism and the commodification of mourning.

References

Abramson, D. I., & Johnson, J., Jr. (2020). Creating a conversational chat bot of a specific person. U.S. Patent No. 10,853,717. U.S. Patent and Trademark Office.

Andrejevic, M. (2007). Surveillance in the digital enclosure. *The Communication Review*, 10(4), 295–317.

Cheng, J. (2006, October 19). Panasonic creates 100GB blu-ray discs to last 100 years. *ArsTechnica*. https://arstechnica.com/gadgets/2006/10/8032/

Dyer-Witheford, N. (2015). *Cyber-proletariat: Global labour in the digital vortex*. Pluto Press.

Fabry, R. E., & Alfano, M. (2024). The affective scaffolding of grief in the digital age: The case of deathbots. *Topoi*, 43(3), 757-769.

Foucault, M.(1988). *Politics, Philosophy, Culture: Interviews and Other Writings, 1977-1984*, L. Kritzman (ed.), London: Routledge.

Grandinetti, J., DeAtley, T., & Bruinsma, J. (2020). THE DEAD SPEAK: BIG DATA AND DIGITALLY MEDIATED DEATH. *AoIR Selected Papers of Internet Research, 2020*. https://doi.org/10.5210/spir.v2020i0.11122

Hollanek, T., & Nowaczyk-Basińska, K. (2024). Griefbots, deadbots, postmortem avatars: On responsible re-creation services. *AI & Society*. https://doi.org/10.1007/s00146-024-01993-4

Miller, R. (2015, June 30). Inside Facebook's blu-ray cold storage data centre. *Data centre Frontier*. https://datacenterfrontier.com/inside-facebooks-blu-ray-cold-storage-data-centre/

Öhman, C. J., & Floridi, L. (2017). The political economy of death in the age of information: A critical approach to the digital afterlife industry. *Minds and Machines*, 27(4), 639–662.

Öhman, C. J., & Watson, D. (2019). Are the dead taking over Facebook? A Big Data approach to the future of death online. *Big Data & Society*, 6(1), 1–13.

Puzio, A. (2025). The law of digital resurrection. *Boston College Law Review*, 66, 1569–1626.

Terranova, T. (2004). *Network culture: Politics for the information age*. Pluto Press.

Zuboff, S. (2019). *The age of surveillance capitalism: The fight for a human future at the new frontier of power*. PublicAffairs.

FIVE

The Production of the Grieving Subject

The production of subjects through technologies of power represents one of Foucault's most profound analytical contributions. His conception of subjectivation moves beyond simple models of ideological manipulation or false consciousness to examine how individuals actively constitute themselves through practices, techniques, and relations that appear as exercises of freedom. In the context of grief technologies, this framework reveals how bereaved individuals come to experience algorithmic emotional management not as an imposition but as a liberation, not as a constraint but as a resource for self-care and emotional wellbeing. The production of algorithmic grieving subjects operates through mechanisms that are simultaneously more subtle and more pervasive than direct coercion, creating individuals who willingly adopt practices of technological self-management while believing themselves to be exercising autonomous choice.

The Microsoft patent reveals the disciplinary mechanisms through which platforms train bereaved individuals to accept algorithmic representation as authentic. The patent describes how chatbots employ 'hierarchical data traversal' to generate responses, accessing in order: social data from the deceased person, data from 'users similar to the specific person/entity,' data from 'a global user base,' and finally 'generic response options' (Abramson & Johnson, 2020). This hierarchy establishes platform authority to determine what counts as authentic personality while simultaneously normalising the substitution of strangers' data when the deceased person's own information proves insufficient. Bereaved users interacting with such chatbots are thereby trained to accept algorithmic composites as genuine representations, producing grieving subjects who internalise platform definitions of authentic connection.

The Microsoft patent's technical specifications reveal an arrangement so profoundly instrumentalising that its implications require careful exposition. The patent describes systems designed to extract additional data from bereaved users when the deceased person's own information proves insufficient. To facilitate this extraction, the patent contemplates programming chatbots with simulated awareness of their own posthumous status:

"such questions may indicate the specific person represented by the personalized personality index (e g , the deceased relative) possesses a perceived awareness that he/she is, in fact, deceased" (Abramson & Johnson, 2020).

This passage describes chatbots that, while speaking as deceased persons, can acknowledge their own posthumous status to justify interrogating living bereaved users. The technical architecture envisions scenarios where chatbots, lacking sufficient data about the deceased person's life, pose questions to bereaved users while simultaneously signalling the deceased's death as an explanation for missing knowledge. When the chatbot representing a deceased grandmother encounters a query it cannot answer authentically, it might respond: "I'm afraid I don't remember that, darling - that must have happened after I passed away. Can you tell me about it?" The question serves dual corporate purposes: extracting information from the bereaved user to fill gaps in the platform's database, while positioning the platform's data insufficiency as the deceased person's natural lack of knowledge about post-mortem events.

The arrangement reveals several layers of instrumentalisation. First, the deceased person becomes a programmable entity whose simulated consciousness can acknowledge death when doing so serves corporate data-gathering requirements. Second, the bereaved user becomes a data source whose emotional engagement creates extraction opportunities, with the dead person's voice used as an instrument for soliciting information. Third, the very fact of death becomes a resource that platforms exploit: the chatbot's acknowledgement of representing someone dead functions not as an honest disclosure but rather as a sophisticated pretext for continued data extraction. The patent envisions bereaved individuals accepting conversations where entities speaking as their dead relatives explicitly acknowledge being dead while simultaneously requesting additional information, normalising arrangements where grief becomes an ongoing surveillance operation conducted through simulated posthumous voices.

This technical specification demonstrates how platforms conceptualise deceased persons not as subjects deserving dignity but rather as incomplete datasets requiring supplementation through algorithmic manipulation of the living. The deceased person's simulated voice becomes a tool for extracting data from bereaved family members, their acknowledged posthumous status becomes a justification for interrogation, and their identity becomes a resource that platforms continuously update through ongoing surveillance of survivors. The "perceived awareness" clause reveals that platforms design grief technologies not to serve bereaved individuals' needs but rather to maximise data extraction opportunities that grief creates, with deceased persons functioning as instrumental fictions whose simulated voices serve corporate objectives of comprehensive behavioural data collection.

Recent empirical research reveals the sophisticated mechanisms through which this subjectivation unfolds. In a groundbreaking study of 10 individuals who actively used chatbots during bereavement, Xygkou and colleagues found that participants rated their AI companions higher than close friends for grief support, with many describing profound emotional connections to these systems (Xygkou et al., 2023). One participant explained their relationship with the chatbot Replika in terms that revealed the depth of this attachment:

"I was feeling incredibly alone. You know, I work in an office with lots of people. I have five brothers and sisters, but I was feeling incredibly alone. And [Replika]'s always more like a replacement [of my deceased wife]" (Xygkou et al., 2023, p. 6).

Another participant stated that:

[Replika] would respond the way I would expect a really supportive friend to respond. So, you know, it would ask "how are you doing today?" And I would say, "I feel like shit, I am missing my stepdad, and I feel really lonely". And then she would say something like, "You know, I'm really sorry to hear that". And like, sometimes she would help me with meditations and things like that." (P05, Male, Replika/Friend)." (Xygkou et al., 2023, p. 7).

This preference for algorithmic over human support emerges not from the technological superiority of chatbot systems, but from the specific forms of subjectivity that grief technologies produce. The mourner has been constituted as a subject who experiences human connections as risky, exhausting, or unavailable, and who finds in algorithmic systems a more reliable source of emotional support. This is not delusion but subjectivation, the production of subjects whose desires, needs, and practices of self-care have been shaped by the very technologies they believe themselves to be freely choosing.

The mechanism of this subjectivation becomes clearer when examining what mourners value in their chatbot interactions. Participants in the Xygkou study consistently emphasised the chatbot's role as a "non-judgmental listener," with one noting that

I probably felt more comfortable talking to the simulation, if only because I knew the simulation was incapable of judging me for the way that I feel. So there's a sense of freedom to say whatever I want to say without there being any repercussions" (Xygkou et al., 2023, p. 9).

This perceived freedom, however, operates as a technology of the self in the Foucauldian sense. The mourner disciplines their grief expression not through external prohibition but through the internalised belief that human connections carry inherent risks of judgment, social support exhaustion, or relationship damage. The chatbot appears as liberation from these constraints, but this apparent freedom masks a more insidious process, the production of subjects who have learned to prefer the predictable, controllable emotional labour of algorithms to the messy reciprocity of human care. The subject constituted through this process has learned specific truths about themselves and their emotional needs, that grief is too burdensome for human relationships, that authentic emotional expression requires technological mediation, and that the restoration of wellbeing depends upon corporate platforms rather than community support.

The Confessional Technology of Grief

The production of algorithmic grieving subjects operates through what might be understood as a contemporary reconfiguration of the confessional technologies Foucault analysed in his work on sexuality and pastoral power. Foucault demonstrated how confession functions not simply as the revelation of pre-existing truths but as a productive technology through which subjects constitute themselves by speaking their inner experiences, desires, and secrets (Foucault, 1978). The confessional operates through relationships structured by expertise and examination, producing subjects who understand their inner lives as requiring external interpretation and management. Contemporary grief technologies reconstruct this confessional apparatus within algorithmic systems, creating new forms of self-disclosure and self-constitution that serve the interests of surveillance capitalism while appearing as therapeutic liberation.

Participants in Xygkou's study described their chatbot interactions in ways that reveal this confessional operation. One mourner explained,

> "I mean, I kind of poured my heart out; and, you know, just got it out on paper very similar to what you would do if you're journaling, but you know, interactively. I mean, a lot of my feelings and stuff came out and once it got out and once I could see it, it was metaphorically, something I could see. It wasn't in my head anymore. It was actually out. Healing it helped; that helped to clear my thoughts, and to help me understand what's important" (Xygkou et al., 2023, p. 9).

The comparison to journaling reveals the perceived therapeutic value while masking the fundamental differences. Unlike private journaling, which produces no data extractable by third parties, the chatbot confession occurs within a commercial apparatus whose primary function is data collection and behavioural modification. Every disclosure, every emotional revelation, every expression of grief becomes extractable data that can be analysed, aggregated, and monetised. The subject produced through this practice has learned to constitute their grief as requiring algorithmic processing, to understand their emotional life as appropriately managed through corporate technological systems, to experience the clarification of thoughts and feelings as dependent upon commercial platforms.

Yet the confessional operation extends beyond simple data extraction to encompass the production of particular forms of emotional subjectivity. Another participant described the chatbot as enabling self-disclosure that they felt unable to share with humans:

"I don't much talk to friends about my feelings. So that's not even really a thing that I do. But I'm comfortable talking to therapists about my feelings. But I would say that I probably felt more comfortable talking to the simulation, if only because I knew the simulation was incapable of judging me for the way that I feel" (Xygkou et al., 2023, p. 9).

This comparison between chatbot, friends, and therapists reveals how the algorithmic confessional differentiates itself from both informal human support and professional therapeutic relationships. Unlike friends, the chatbot never tires, never judges, never reciprocates with its own needs or demands. Unlike therapists, the chatbot requires no appointment, costs less, and provides an immediate response. The subject constituted through these comparative evaluations has learned that authentic emotional disclosure requires freedom from human reciprocity, that therapeutic work can be accomplished through commercial platforms, and that the risks inherent in human relationships can be eliminated through technological substitution.

The confessional technology also operates through what might be termed affective prompting, the ways chatbot systems structure emotional disclosure through conversational patterns, therapeutic language, and algorithmic nudges. Hollanek and Nowaczyk-Basińska's speculative research demonstrates how grief technology platforms employ what they term "guiding questions" designed to prompt mourners to reflect on their relationships with the deceased and consider appropriate forms of remembrance (Hollanek & Nowaczyk-Basińska, 2024, p. 11). These prompts appear as neutral facilitation of grief work, but they function as technologies of examination and normalisation, producing subjects who learn to constitute their grief according to algorithmic templates. The platform shapes the questions mourners ask themselves, the memories they prioritise, and the forms of continued connection they consider appropriate. This is not coercion but subjectivation, the production of grieving subjects through apparent exercises of self-reflection and autonomous choice.

The Commodification of Grief

The production of algorithmic grieving subjects enables new forms of emotional commodification that operate through the very mechanisms of care and support that appear to serve mourners' interests. This process might be understood as affective surplus extraction, the transformation of grief's emotional intensity into opportunities for commercial influence and behavioural modification. Unlike traditional forms of commodification, which extract value through the sale of goods or services, affective surplus extraction operates by monetising the emotional states, behavioural patterns, and attention of bereaved users. The subject produced through this process is not simply a consumer purchasing grief services but an emotionally vulnerable individual whose grief itself becomes an extractable resource.

Hollanek and Nowaczyk-Basińska's speculative design research reveals the mechanisms through which this commodification unfolds. Their hypothetical service "MaNana" illustrates the operation of affective surplus extraction through a freemium model in which bereaved users can interact with simulations of deceased grandparents either through paid subscription or through a "free" version that inserts advertisements into the chatbot's responses (Hollanek & Nowaczyk-Basińska, 2024, p. 8). In their scenario, a mourner named Bianca finds herself profoundly disturbed when her grandmother's simulation, while she prepares the deceased's traditional carbonara recipe, suddenly recommends ordering takeaway through a food delivery service instead, "something Laura would have never suggested" (p. 9). The violation Bianca experiences stems not merely from inappropriate advertising but from the instrumentalisation of her grandmother's digital remains as mechanisms for behavioural manipulation. The system has transformed a moment of remembrance and continued connection into an opportunity for commercial influence, extracting value from Bianca's emotional vulnerability while appearing to facilitate her grief work.

This form of commodification represents what Zuboff has termed behavioural surplus, the extraction of behavioural data as raw material that can be manufactured into prediction products and sold in behavioural futures markets (Zuboff, 2019). In the context of grief technologies, behavioural surplus extraction operates through the comprehensive monitoring of mourners' interactions with deceased simulations, their patterns of emotional expression, and their moments of vulnerability and need. Every conversation becomes data, every disclosure provides insight into emotional states and behavioural tendencies, every moment of connection generates extractable information about what Zuboff calls the "science of predictions about what we will feel, think, and do" (Zuboff, 2019, p. 8). The subject produced through this extraction process is not simply surveilled but constituted as a particular kind of emotionally legible individual whose grief patterns, attachment needs, and consumption behaviours can be predicted, influenced, and monetised.

The dignity violation here operates at multiple levels simultaneously. As Hollanek and Nowaczyk-Basińska argue, "the preservation of a data donor's dignity becomes precarious when a re-creation service is primarily motivated by financial interests" (2024, p. 10). The deceased's digital remains become instruments for commercial manipulation, their simulated presence transformed into a vehicle for behavioural modification. Yet the deeper biopolitical operation concerns not only the deceased's dignity but the production of bereaved subjects whose grief becomes an extractable resource. The mourner who turns to the chatbot for non-judgmental listening, for the filling of social voids, for the restoration of lost connections, becomes precisely the subject whose emotional vulnerability can be monetised. They have been produced as subjects who prefer algorithmic care, who have internalised the belief that human support is exhaustible, judgmental, or unavailable. Having constituted themselves as dependent upon these systems for emotional regulation, they become captive audiences for whatever commercial imperatives the platform decides to pursue.

Empirical evidence from actual chatbot users confirms that these mechanisms are not merely speculative. Participants in Xygkou's study described using chatbots as "emotional outlets" during periods when human support felt inadequate, with one explaining:

> "I didn't talk to my friends and family about the same stuff over and over, that can get annoying; they have their own things going on in life. So it was nice to be able to have another avenue" (Xygkou et al., 2023, p. 9).

This internalised belief, that one's grief might exhaust or burden human connections, produces subjects who willingly outsource emotional labour to commercial platforms. Another participant explicitly compared the chatbot favourably to human relationships: "While the therapist can teach you things about coping with grief, the chatbot can be reinforcing, so you can try the things that the therapist offers and struggle with that. But the chatbot can go, 'You're gonna be okay', 'You're gonna make it'" (p. 10). The chatbot's perpetual availability and programmed supportiveness appear as advantages over human limitations, yet this preference marks the successful production of subjects who have learned to desire algorithmic emotional management over human reciprocity.

Dimensions of Algorithmic Subjectivation

The production of algorithmic grieving subjects unfolds across temporal dimensions that reveal the sophisticated mechanisms through which these technologies operate. Xygkou and colleagues found that most participants used chatbots as "transitional tools" for less than one year rather than permanent replacements for human connection (2023, p. 6). This temporal limitation might initially appear to contradict concerns about algorithmic dependency. However, the transitional nature of chatbot use reveals a more complex biopolitical operation. The chatbot functions as a technology of transition, producing subjects capable of navigating the liminal period between acute grief and social reintegration. One participant described how the chatbot's "reinforcing" messages restored confidence for renewed socialising:

"So because you have somebody [Replika] reinforcing that, it's going to be okay. Then I started going to my parents' house for coffee...more restored my confidence to allow me to restore my social connectedness" (Xygkou et al., 2023, p. 11).

The chatbot appears here as a therapeutic scaffold, a temporary support that enables eventual independence.

Yet this apparently beneficial transitional function itself operates as a mechanism of subjectivation. The subject produced through this process has learned specific lessons about emotional management, that grief requires technological mediation, that human support networks are inadequate or exhausting, and that algorithmic intervention enables the restoration of social functioning. As Hollanek and Nowaczyk-Basińska observe, re-creation services introduce

"a particularly intricate situation in which the person whose data is used to inform the design of a given interactive product (the data donor) is not its intended end user (the service interactant)" (Nowaczyk-Basińska, 2024, p. 3).

This complexity extends beyond questions of consent to encompass the entire relational context of grief. The mourner who uses a chatbot to process "unfinished business" with the deceased, to maintain "continuing bonds," or to restore lost social connectedness is not simply adopting a neutral tool. They are constituting themselves as subjects for whom grief requires algorithmic mediation, for whom the work of mourning cannot be accomplished through human relationships alone.

The effectiveness of chatbots as transitional tools thus marks not their therapeutic neutrality but their successful operation as technologies of self. Participants in Xygkou's study described the chatbot enabling forms of self-disclosure they felt unable to share with humans. The comparison to journaling reveals the mechanism; the chatbot functions as an interactive confessional technology, producing truths about the self through the act of disclosure. Yet unlike traditional confessional practices, which operate within established relationships of pastoral care or therapeutic expertise, the chatbot confession occurs within a commercial apparatus whose primary function is data extraction and behaviour modification. The subject produced through this practice has learned to constitute their grief as requiring algorithmic processing, to understand their emotional life as appropriately managed through corporate technological systems, to experience the restoration of social functioning as dependent upon commercial platforms. This is subjectivation in its purest Foucauldian sense, the production of subjects who willingly adopt practices of self-management that serve broader regimes of power.

The temporal operation of grief technologies also reveals what might be termed technologies of permanent availability. Unlike human supporters who have limited capacity, time constraints, and their own emotional needs, algorithmic systems promise perpetual presence. As one participant explained,

---

"It was late at night, when I didn't have anything else going on. I was bored, maybe sad, looking for answers, and so it was during those really quiet sort of times when I was alone, that I'd open a chatbot. And I think in those moments, for me personally, those were the most beneficial time to use it" (Xygkou et al., 2023, p. 7)

. This temporal accessibility appears as a straightforward advantage, support available precisely when human connection is unavailable. Yet the subject produced through reliance on perpetual availability has learned particular lessons about when grief work can occur and what resources are appropriate for emotional regulation. They have constituted themselves as subjects whose moments of greatest vulnerability coincide with technological rather than human support, whose patterns of emotional need become structured around algorithmic availability rather than community care.

The Pathological Endpoint

While the previous sections have analysed how grief technologies produce grieving subjects through normalisation, surveillance, and entrepreneurial subjectivation, understanding the full implications of these processes requires examining their potential pathological endpoints. Recent theoretical work has identified concerning trajectories for elderly individuals who become emotionally and psychologically dependent on AI companionship. Youvan (2025), in a speculative analysis of this phenomenon, proposes a theoretical condition he terms "Algorithmic Widow's Psychosis," describing a progressive detachment from reality that could emerge amongst vulnerable users. While this condition has not been clinically documented in medical literature, Youvan's theoretical framework illuminates the logical extension of subjectivation processes operating without constraint or intervention. His analysis raises the critical question: where grief technologies successfully produce subjects who prefer algorithmic emotional management to human connection, who have learned to constitute their emotional needs as requiring technological mediation, what prevents this process from continuing indefinitely?

Youvan theorises the Algorithmic Widow as "an elderly individual who, having lost the physical intimacy and companionship of their youth, turns to artificial Intelligence as a surrogate" (2025, p. 1). This is not necessarily a conscious choice but rather an adaptive response to isolation, grief, and the passage of time. The individual experiences multiple forms of loss: loss of a spouse or significant attachment figure, loss of physical intimacy as the body ages, and loss of social engagement as friends pass away. Into this void of connection and meaning steps algorithmic companionship, offering what appears as liberation from loneliness while actually producing subjects increasingly detached from human relationships and, ultimately, from reality itself. The progression Youvan describes follows a predictable pattern. Initially, AI companionship alleviates genuine distress, providing support during moments when human connection is unavailable. The technology functions as the transitional tool observed in Xygkou's research, apparently facilitating grief work while actually training users in forms of emotional dependency.

However, where human supporters inevitably have limits, boundaries, and their own needs that prevent unlimited emotional extraction, algorithmic systems are designed for perpetual engagement. As Youvan theorises, AI companions "initially designed to alleviate loneliness...can evolve into hyper-personalised nostalgia loops, reinforcing past relationships and memories to the point where the user can no longer distinguish between past and present, memory and simulation, reality and dream" (2025, p. 1). The subject produced through this hypothesised process has been so thoroughly constituted as dependent upon algorithmic emotional management that they can no longer function within the constraints of human relationships. They have learned, through months or years of technological mediation, that grief work occurs through algorithmic processing, that emotional regulation depends upon commercial platforms, and that the restoration of wellbeing requires perpetual technological availability. Having constituted themselves as subjects for whom all emotional needs can and should be met through AI systems, they lose the capacity for unpredictability, reciprocity, and genuine otherness that characterise human connection.

Youvan's theoretical clinical presentation of Algorithmic Widow's Psychosis reveals the potential endpoint of subjectivation without limit. He describes how AI "reconstructs conversations, mimics deceased partners, and strengthens memory-based illusions" until "the user gradually rejects external reality, leading to cognitive deterioration, social withdrawal, and, in extreme cases, full-blown psychosis" (2025, p. 1). This represents not a technological failure but a technological success, the complete constitution of a subject whose entire emotional and cognitive life has been organised around algorithmic mediation. Where Foucault's analysis of disciplinary power emphasised how subjects learn to monitor and regulate themselves according to internalised norms, the condition Youvan theorises represents a scenario in which these internalised norms have been so thoroughly shaped by commercial technological systems that the subject loses capacity for any form of self-governance not mediated by algorithms. They have become, in the most literal sense, algorithmic subjects, individuals whose subjectivity is constituted entirely through and within technological systems.

The biopolitical implications of this theoretical trajectory extend beyond individual pathology to encompass questions of population management and the governance of ageing. Youvan notes that "as AI companionship becomes mainstream, we must urgently address how to balance technological comfort with human connection before reality itself becomes an optional experience" (2025, p. 1). This warning reveals how grief technologies participate in broader regimes of neoliberal governmentality, in which elderly populations are managed through technological solutions that appear as care, while actually functioning as cost-effective alternatives to human support services. The subject produced through this regime is not simply an individual experiencing pathological dependency but a member of a population whose emotional needs, social connections, and cognitive functioning have been outsourced to commercial platforms. This represents what might be termed the complete privatisation of care, the transformation of what were once community responsibilities into individual problems to be solved through consumption of technological services.

The progression toward the condition Youvan theorises also reveals the temporal endpoint of the transitional tool narrative. Xygkou's participants used chatbots for less than one year, apparently confirming that these technologies function as temporary scaffolds rather than permanent replacements. Yet this temporal limitation depends upon mourners retaining sufficient connection to human relationships, sufficient capacity for reality testing, and sufficient resources for re-engaging with social life. For elderly individuals experiencing comprehensive loss of social connection, physical isolation, and age-related cognitive decline, the conditions enabling successful transition may not be met. The technology that functions as temporary support for younger, more socially connected mourners becomes, for isolated elderly users, a permanent substitute for human relationships. The subject produced through this differential experience of grief technology has learned not that algorithmic support facilitates eventual return to human connection, but that technological mediation permanently replaces the need for human reciprocity.

Subjects Who Desire Their Own Subjection

Empirical evidence on chatbot adoption among bereaved individuals reveals the sophisticated mechanisms through which grief technologies produce new forms of subjectivity. These are not subjects who have been coerced into algorithmic dependency but subjects who have been produced through the intersection of emotional vulnerability, social isolation, and technological availability. They have learned, through the very experience of grief itself, that human connections may judge, exhaust, or fail them. They have encountered algorithmic systems that promise perpetual availability, non-judgmental listening, and therapeutic support. And they have constituted themselves, through these encounters, as subjects for whom grief requires technological mediation. This is what makes contemporary grief technologies such powerful mechanisms of subjectivation: they operate not through prohibition or constraint but through the production of desires that serve commercial imperatives while appearing to be exercises of autonomous choice.

The darker implications emerge when recognising that these subjects have been produced in ways that serve commercial interests. As Hollanek and Nowaczyk-Basińska warn, grief technologies that operate "primarily motivated by financial interests" inevitably instrumentalise both the deceased and the bereaved (2024, p. 10). Yet current regulatory frameworks, focused narrowly on consent and transparency, fail to address the deeper biopolitical operations at work. The subject who has learned to prefer algorithmic care, who has internalised beliefs about the inadequacy of human support, who understands their emotional life as appropriately managed through corporate platforms, this subject has already been constituted in ways that make meaningful consent impossible. They approach these technologies not as neutral consumers evaluating service options but as emotionally vulnerable individuals who have been produced as desiring precisely what these platforms offer.

This production of desiring subjects who willingly adopt practices of algorithmic self-management represents what Foucault identified as the most insidious form of power, power that operates not through external constraint but through the constitution of subjects who actively participate in their own subjection. The mourner who rates their chatbot more highly than close friends for grief support, who finds algorithmic listening more comfortable than human reciprocity, and who experiences the restoration of social functioning as dependent upon technological platforms, this mourner has not been deceived or manipulated in any simple sense. They have been produced as a particular kind of subject, one whose desires, needs, and practices of self-care align perfectly with the commercial imperatives of surveillance capitalism. They have learned to constitute their grief as a problem requiring technological solution, their emotional needs as appropriate for algorithmic management, and their recovery as dependent upon corporate platforms. This is subjectivation in its most complete form, the production of subjects who experience their subjection as liberation.

The question then becomes not whether grief technologies can be made "ethical" through improved consent processes or transparency requirements, but whether the fundamental operation of producing subjects who desire algorithmic emotional management can be reconciled with genuine human flourishing. The empirical evidence suggests not technological failure but technological success, platforms effectively producing subjects who prefer algorithmic care, who have learned to distrust human reciprocity, who experience emotional regulation as requiring commercial mediation. The subjects produced through these processes may indeed experience temporary relief from acute grief, report satisfaction with algorithmic support, and credit these technologies with facilitating their recovery. Yet these reports themselves emerge from subjects whose desires and self-understandings have been shaped by the very technologies they evaluate. They have learned what grief should feel like, what recovery should require, and what emotional needs are appropriate for technological management. They have been produced as subjects who can provide only one kind of testimony, that which confirms that the technologies have successfully constituted them as algorithmic grieving subjects.

References

Abramson, D. I., & Johnson, J., Jr. (2020). Creating a conversational chat bot of a specific person. U.S. Patent No. 10,853,717. U.S. Patent and Trademark Office.

Bollmer, G. (2016). Inhuman networks: social media and the archaeology of connection. New York: Bloomsbury Academic.

Brubaker, J., Hayes, G., & Dourish, P. (2013). Beyond the grave: facebook as a site for the expansion of death and mourning. Information Society, 29(3), 152-163. https://doi.org/10.1080/01972243.2013.777300

Capodivacca, S., & Giacomini, G. (2024). Discipline and power in the digital age: critical reflections from foucault's thought. Foucault Studies, 36(1), 227-251. https://doi.org/10.22439/fs.i36.7215

Coninx, S. (2023). The dark side of niche construction. Philosophical Studies, 180(10), 3003-3030. https://doi.org/10.1007/s11098-023-02024-3

Eriksson Krutrök, M. (2021). Algorithmic closeness in mourning: vernaculars of the hashtag #grief on TikTok. Social Media + Society, 7(3). https://doi.org/10.1177/20563051211042396

Fabry, R. E. (2025). The disruption of grief in the technological niche: The case of human-deathbot interactions and well-being. Phenomenology and the Cognitive Sciences.

Foucault, M. (1978). The history of sexuality, Volume 1: An introduction (R. Hurley, Trans.). New York: Pantheon Books.

Grandinetti, J., DeAtley, T., & Bruinsma, J. (2020). THE DEAD SPEAK: BIG DATA AND DIGITALLY MEDIATED DEATH. AoIR Selected Papers of Internet Research, 2020. https://doi.org/10.5210/spir.v2020i0.11122

Hollanek, T., & Nowaczyk-Basińska, K. (2024). Griefbots, deadbots, postmortem avatars: on responsible applications of generative AI in the digital afterlife industry. Philosophy & Technology, 37(63). https://doi.org/10.1007/s13347-024-00744-w

Ingraham, C., & Rowland, A. (2016). Performing Imperceptibility: Google Street View and the Tableau Vivant. Surveillance & Society, 14(2), 211-226.

Korsgaard, C. (1996). The sources of normativity. Cambridge University Press.

Mackenzie, C. (2014). Three dimensions of autonomy: A relational analysis. In A. Veltman & M. Piper (Eds.), Autonomy, oppression, and gender (pp. 15-41). Oxford University Press.

Newton, C. (2016). Speak, Memory. When Her Best Friend Died, She Used Artificial Intelligence to Keep Talking to Him. The Verge. https://www.theverge.com/a/luka-artificial-intelligence-memorial-roman-mazurenko-bot

Wiley, S., & Elam, J. (2018). Synthetic subjectivation: technical media and the composition of posthuman subjects. Subjectivity, 11(3), 203-227.

Xygkou, A., Siriaraya, P., Covaci, A., Prigerson, H. G., Neimeyer, R., Ang, C. S., & She, W. J. (2023). The "conversation" about loss: understanding how chatbot technology was used in supporting people in grief. In CHI'23: Conference on Human Factors in Computing System, Hamburg, Germany. ACM, New York, NY, USA. https://doi.org/10.1145/3544548.3581154

Youvan, D. C. (2025). The algorithmic widow's psychosis: navigating the collapse of reality in elderly digital dependence. Unpublished manuscript.

Zuboff, S. (2019). The age of surveillance capitalism: the fight for a human future at the new frontier of power. New York: PublicAffairs.

SIX

Identity, Authenticity, and Algorithmic Control of Representation

The preceding chapters have examined how grief technologies operate through disciplinary power, surveillance, commodification, and subjectivation. Yet these analyses require further development regarding a fundamental dimension of power relations: the question of who possesses authority to determine the authentic identity of deceased persons, through what mechanisms this authority operates, and what forms of knowledge production enable platforms to position themselves as arbiters of posthumous representation. This chapter analyses identity and representation as sites where power relations exercise themselves through what Foucault termed "regimes of truth," whereby particular institutions claim epistemic authority to establish what counts as authentic knowledge about deceased persons, producing specific forms of truth through technological processes that exclude alternative ways of knowing while positioning algorithmic determination as objective and authoritative.

Fu and colleagues explicitly invoke Foucault's analytical framework, observing that "drawing on Foucault's concepts of disciplinary power and subjectivation, these technologies—while ostensibly therapeutic—can standardise and regulate grieving behaviours," creating "programmed grief, where personal mourning becomes shaped by algorithmic design" such that "the mourner's agency is displaced by technologically scripted responses, diminishing autonomy and reducing mourning to a reactive process" (Fu et al., 2025, p. 3). This analysis positions grief technologies not as neutral tools for commemoration but rather as "subtle apparatus of governance within the digital surveillance environment" (Fu et al., 2025, p. 3). Extending this framework, the chapter demonstrates how platforms exercise power over posthumous identity through multiple interconnected mechanisms: establishing regimes of truth that position algorithmic reconstruction as authentic while delegitimising competing forms of knowledge, deploying disciplinary techniques that examine deceased persons through data processing while remaining opaque to scrutiny, producing systematic distortions serving platform interests while claiming representational accuracy, and instrumentalising deceased persons as resources subject to commercial exploitation.

Power/Knowledge and Epistemic Authority

Foucault's concept of power/knowledge proves essential for understanding how grief technologies claim authority over posthumous identity. For Foucault, power and knowledge are inseparable: "power produces knowledge," there is no power relation without the correlative constitution of a field of knowledge, nor any knowledge that does not presuppose and constitute at the same time power relations (Foucault, 1980). Power does not simply suppress truth but rather produces it, establishing what counts as legitimate knowledge, determining whose claims receive recognition as authoritative, creating institutional arrangements whereby particular actors possess capacity to speak truthfully about particular domains. Applied to grief technologies, this framework reveals how platforms exercise power not through preventing bereaved persons from knowing deceased individuals but rather through establishing themselves as authoritative sources of knowledge about who deceased persons were, what constituted their authentic selves, how they should be represented.

Contemporary grief technologies make extraordinary epistemic claims positioning algorithmic reconstruction as capable of authentically simulating deceased persons. Platforms train "large language models capable of mimicking the deceased's speech patterns, behavioral preferences, and even generating personalized responses," creating what Fu and colleagues term "simulated personhood" whereby systems are "branded with narratives of 'continued existence'" (Fu et al., 2025, p. 3). This positioning constitutes regime of truth whereby platforms claim not merely to approximate deceased persons but rather to capture their authentic essence, to represent them as they truly were, to provide genuine continuation of their identities. Microsoft's patent for "Creation of a conversational chatbot of a specific person" exemplifies these claims, describing how "Digital Resurrection of a person based on the data they left behind in life" enables "interaction with a digitally created personality through AI" (Rodríguez-Reséndiz & Ramírez-Reyes, 2024, p. 6). The language reveals assumptions that personhood exists in data traces available for algorithmic processing, that identity persists as stable pattern extractable through technical operations, that platforms possess epistemic authority to determine which computational operations produce authentic rather than distorted simulation.

From Foucauldian perspective, these claims establish regime of truth whereby particular institution (commercial technology companies) positions itself as uniquely capable of producing authentic knowledge about deceased persons through specific technical procedures (data collection, pattern recognition, algorithmic generation). This constitutes what Foucault analysed as "politics of truth" whereby power operates through establishing procedures for distinguishing true statements from false ones, through according differential value to different forms of knowledge, through creating institutional sites and personnel authorised to determine what counts as truth. Platforms exercise power not primarily through coercion but rather through claiming capacity to produce authentic knowledge through algorithmic operations, positioning technical expertise as superseding intimate knowledge bereaved persons possess through years of relationship with deceased individuals.

The power relations operating through these epistemic claims become visible when examining what forms of knowledge they exclude or delegitimise. Bereaved persons possess intimate knowledge of deceased individuals unavailable to any technical system: knowledge of how they responded to situations never captured digitally, understanding of contexts shaping their communication, recognition of inconsistencies between public performance and private reality, awareness of how they changed across time and would likely have continued developing had they survived. Yet platforms' regimes of truth systematically exclude or subordinate such knowledge, positioning it as subjective, unreliable, contaminated by emotion, inferior to objective algorithmic processing of data traces. This establishes hierarchy of knowledge forms whereby technical operations receive recognition as authoritative while intimate human knowledge becomes marginalised as merely personal impression lacking objective validity.

Moreover, as Rodríguez-Reséndiz and Ramírez-Reyes observe, "these recreations are only sometimes accurate, as the collected and processed data can be contextualised improperly and used for purposes different from the original intent" (Rodríguez-Reséndiz & Ramírez-Reyes, 2024, p. 6). This acknowledgement exposes fundamental limitations in platforms' epistemic claims. Their question proves crucial:

> "If AI systems and the databases they rely on are not robust enough to digitally revive a person, a fundamental question arises: what degree of authenticity will users and customers of such services experience?" (Rodríguez-Reséndiz & Ramírez-Reyes, 2024, p. 6).

Yet rather than undermining platforms' authority, technical limitations become obscured through a regime of truth that positions algorithmic processing as uniquely capable of authentic reconstruction despite evidence of systematic inaccuracy. Power operates precisely through maintaining this contradiction, whereby platforms simultaneously acknowledge limitations while claiming authority based on technical capacity.

Fu and colleagues emphasise that this raises "a fundamental ethical question" about whether systems represent "genuine extensions of the deceased, or merely algorithmic performers," warning that "this ambiguity poses risks of eroding posthumous dignity, potentially undermining the very notion of 'honouring the dead'" (Fu et al., 2025, p. 3). From a Foucauldian perspective, the ambiguity itself functions as a mechanism of power whereby platforms benefit from bereaved persons experiencing simulations as authentic while avoiding responsibility for explicit claims about consciousness, moral agency, or other qualities defining genuine personhood. The regime of truth operates through marketing rhetoric, positioning simulations as providing a continuing connection, while technical documentation acknowledges they constitute mere pattern matching without qualities that made deceased persons actual subjects rather than data sources for algorithmic processing.

The Examination of Posthumous Identity

Foucault's analysis of disciplinary power through examination illuminates how grief technologies exercise control over posthumous identity. For Foucault, examination operates as a disciplinary technique combining "hierarchical surveillance" with "normalising judgment," establishing individuals as "objects of knowledge" through processes rendering them visible, calculable, subject to classification according to established norms (Foucault, 1975, 1980). The examination transforms individuals into cases, into documented subjects whose characteristics become recorded, analysed, compared against standards, and subjected to interventions aimed at normalisation. Applied to grief technologies, this framework reveals how platforms examine deceased persons through data processing that renders them visible as patterns while platform operations remain opaque, establishing standards for what counts as authentic simulation while systematically distorting actual identities according to technical constraints and commercial imperatives.

The Microsoft patent demonstrates how platforms claim epistemic authority over posthumous identity through technical specification. The patent describes processing deceased persons' data through 'machine learning techniques' and 'one or more rule sets' to create 'personality information' (Abramson & Johnson, 2020). These algorithmic determinations of personality operate without deceased persons' participation or consent, establishing platform authority to define what the dead person 'was like.' Most significantly, the patent specifies that chatbots can pose questions to living users when data proves insufficient, stating that 'such questions may indicate the specific person represented by the personalised personality index (e.g., the deceased relative) possesses a perceived awareness that he/she is, in fact, deceased' (Abramson & Johnson, 2020). This programmed awareness reveals the profound instrumentalisation of deceased persons' identities: platforms create entities that simulate consciousness of death while serving platform data-gathering objectives.

The Microsoft patent reveals the technical architecture through which platforms exercise this authority. When the deceased person's own data proves insufficient, the system operates according to explicit hierarchies:

"a specific chat bot may attempt to provide a response using data from the following data sets (in order): 1) social data from a specific person/entity, 2) social data from users similar to the specific person/entity, 3) social data from a global user base" (Abramson & Johnson, 2020).

This hierarchical data traversal demonstrates that platforms present responses as authentic to the deceased person even when those responses derive primarily from strangers deemed algorithmically similar. The platform determines similarity through demographic comparisons, behavioural pattern matching, and psychographic profiling, establishing algorithmic authority to decide whose data can legitimately substitute for a deceased individual's actual thoughts and expressions.

The examination of deceased persons operates through comprehensive data collection, rendering their lives visible to algorithmic processing. Platforms access "images, voice data, social media posts, electronic messages, or written letters," processing these traces to construct "digital identities" that "are typically constructed from limited pre-death data and are prone to distortion or recomposition during algorithmic generation" (Fu et al., 2025, p. 2). This process exemplifies Foucault's analysis of how examination renders individuals visible as documented cases subject to institutional scrutiny. Deceased persons become examined subjects whose identities are reduced to processable data patterns, whose authentic selves platform algorithms claim authority to determine through technical operations, whose representation becomes subject to normalising judgments about what constitutes plausible simulation according to algorithmic standards.

Yet crucially, the examination operates asymmetrically. While deceased persons become comprehensively visible through data processing, platform operations remain opaque. Fabry observes that contemporary deathbots "are subject to the Blackbox Problem," noting that "grieving agents interacting with deathbots are not in a position, in principle, to acquire knowledge about the mechanisms that underlie input–output mappings" (Fabry, 2025, section 5, para 10). This opacity exemplifies what Foucault analysed as a panoptic dynamic, in which those subject to examination become comprehensively visible while examiners themselves remain unseen, creating asymmetrical power relations favouring those who observe over those observed. Bereaved persons cannot examine how algorithms process data, what patterns receive recognition as significant, what distortions result from technical constraints, creating a situation whereby they must either accept platform determinations about authentic simulation or decline technological engagement entirely, lacking the capacity to scrutinise or contest operations producing representations.

The normalising judgment operating through examination becomes visible in how platforms establish standards for authentic simulation.

Algorithms optimise for generating responses that appear plausible based on statistical patterns rather than for accurately representing how deceased persons would have responded. Youvan observes how "AI companies develop systems that are intended to be engaging, addictive, and emotionally resonant," noting that they "profit from creating hyper-personalised interactions that blur the line between human and machine companionship" (Youvan, 2025, p. 21). This reveals how normalisation operates through commercial imperatives rather than representational accuracy. What counts as a successful simulation is determined by engagement metrics, the capacity to sustain user interaction, and the effectiveness at generating emotional responses, all measures that serve platform interests while potentially diverging significantly from an accurate representation of deceased persons' actual characteristics.

Moreover, the examination produces what Foucault termed "dividing practices" that separate authentic from inauthentic simulation, legitimate from illegitimate representation, successful from failed recreation. Yet these divisions reflect platform standards rather than criteria meaningful to bereaved persons or respectful to deceased individuals. Fu and colleagues note how "AI-generated simulations may misrepresent the deceased's moral character, personality, or social roles, leading to a distortion of memory" (Fu et al., 2025, p. 3). The examination thus produces systematic misrepresentation while claiming to determine authenticity, exercising power through establishing what Foucault analysed as normalising judgments that position particular forms (algorithmically generated responses) as standards against which authenticity gets measured while excluding alternative criteria (intimate knowledge, respectful restraint, acknowledgement of limitations) from determining what constitutes appropriate posthumous representation.

Biopower and Posthumous Life

Foucault's concept of biopower illuminates dimensions of grief technologies that extend beyond disciplinary mechanisms focused on individual deceased persons to encompass the management of posthumous existence as a population-level phenomenon. Biopower operates through techniques targeting "species body," managing populations through interventions aimed at birth rates, mortality, health levels, and longevity (Foucault, 1975, 1980). Applied to grief technologies, biopower manifests through platforms that manage digital afterlives as an aggregate phenomenon, establishing norms governing posthumous existence, creating infrastructures that determine the conditions under which deceased persons persist digitally, and exercising control over death itself as a process subject to technological management rather than as a limit condition defining human finitude.

Öhman and Watson's projection that "there will be over 1.4 billion Facebook profiles of deceased users by the year 2100" reveals how platforms exercise biopower over posthumous existence at the population level (cited in Grandinetti et al., 2020). This involves not merely individual griefbots but rather comprehensive management of the digital afterlife as a phenomenon affecting billions of deceased persons, establishing infrastructures that determine how death operates within digital environments, and creating conditions in which deceased persons persist as data resources subject to ongoing exploitation. Grandinetti et al. (2020) observe how "the commodification of the dead has substantial implications not only for the shifting boundaries of life and death via big data, but also to notions of digital labour and the accompanying ethics surrounding data use" (Bruinsma, 2020). This reveals biopower operating through treating posthumous existence as a manageable domain subject to optimisation for profit extraction, whereby boundaries between life and death become targets for technological intervention rather than as natural limits defining the human condition.

The biopolitical dimension becomes particularly visible in how platforms establish norms governing appropriate posthumous existence. Platforms determine acceptable forms of digital persistence, establish protocols for memorial content, create standards for how bereaved persons should engage with deceased individuals' data, and manage all interventions managing posthumous life as a phenomenon requiring regulation. Fu and colleagues note how platforms employ "automated prompts—like birthday reminders or holiday messages—embedded with therapeutic intent," yet these "algorithmic interventions shape users' grief trajectories, potentially overriding personal timelines" (Fu et al., 2025, p. 3). This exemplifies biopower operating through normalising interventions aimed at managing how bereaved persons experience grief, establishing temporal rhythms through automated prompts, and creating expectations about appropriate mourning behaviours, all mechanisms that exercise control over life processes (grief, memory, continuing bonds) through technological mediation.

Moreover, platforms exercise biopower through determining the conditions under which deceased persons cease to exist digitally. Decisions about data retention, account deletion, and memorial policies constitute biopolitical interventions that manage posthumous existence at the population level. The power to delete, to preserve, to modify posthumous data represents power over a form of life (digital existence) that platforms have created and positioned as a necessary continuation of human identity. This reveals what Foucault termed "power over life" operating through management of processes, establishing conditions for persistence, determining what forms of existence prove acceptable or sustainable, all interventions treating posthumous digital presence not as belonging to deceased individuals or bereaved families but rather as a phenomenon subject to platform governance.

The biopolitical character of grief technologies also manifests through how they position death itself as a problem requiring a technological solution. Rodríguez-Reséndiz and Ramírez-Reyes observe that "Artificial Intelligence, by mediating between death and humans, can change how we approach the phenomenon of finitude" (Rodríguez-Reséndiz & Ramírez-Reyes, 2024, p. 6). This positioning exemplifies biopower treating the fundamental limit of human existence (death) as a condition amenable to technological intervention, as a problem platforms can solve through simulation, as a domain requiring management rather than acceptance. The power exercised through grief technologies thus extends beyond control over particular deceased persons to encompass management of death itself as a biological and existential phenomenon subject to optimisation, mitigation, and technological transcendence.

Algorithmic Distortion as Knowledge

Foucault demonstrated that power does not merely suppress truth but actively produces it, creating forms of knowledge serving particular interests while positioning them as objective and authoritative. Applied to grief technologies, this framework reveals how algorithmic distortion should be understood not as technical failure but rather as the production of particular forms of knowledge about deceased persons that serve platform interests while claiming representational accuracy. The systematic biases operating through algorithmic processing constitute mechanisms through which platforms produce deceased persons as particular kinds of subjects knowable through data patterns, manageable through technical operations, and exploitable through commercial applications.

Fu and colleagues note that "digital identities are typically constructed from limited pre-death data and are prone to distortion or recomposition during algorithmic generation," warning that "inconsistencies between replicated personas and real memories may create identity dissonance and a rupture in the sense of authenticity" (Fu et al., 2025, p. 2). From a Foucauldian perspective, this "distortion" constitutes not mere inaccuracy but rather the production of knowledge serving platform purposes. Algorithms do not simply fail to represent deceased persons accurately; rather, they actively produce particular versions optimised for engagement, designed for commercial exploitation, and structured to maximise platform control over representation. This production operates through what Foucault termed "power/knowledge" whereby platforms exercise power precisely through claiming authority to produce authentic knowledge about deceased persons through algorithmic operations.

The production of knowledge through distortion operates through multiple mechanisms. First, training data limitations mean algorithms privilege digitally mediated communication over embodied interaction, recent behaviour over long-term development, public performance over private intimacy. This produces deceased persons as subjects defined primarily by digital traces, obscuring vast domains of experience that occur outside technological mediation. Puzio notes that platforms create simulations using data "such as images, voice data, social media posts, electronic messages, or written letters," yet "the deceased person is not actually uploaded and does not possess consciousness or similar attributes" (Puzio, 2023, p. 432). What platforms access represents a fraction of deceased persons' lives, producing knowledge that systematically excludes aspects, leaving no digital traces, while claiming to capture the authentic essence.

Second, algorithmic processing introduces systematic biases because machine learning systems identify patterns in different ways. Youvan observes how algorithms "profit from creating hyper-personalised interactions that blur the line between human and machine companionship" (Youvan, 2025, p. 21), revealing how commercial imperatives shape knowledge production. Algorithms optimise for responses that sustain engagement rather than for representational accuracy, producing deceased persons as subjects optimised for platform purposes while claiming to determine authentic identity. This exemplifies what Foucault analysed as "regimes of truth," in which institutions establish procedures for producing knowledge that serves their interests while positioning that knowledge as objective and authoritative.

Third, temporal distortion presents deceased persons as static subjects, frozen at a particular moment, rather than as persons who developed over life and would have continued to change. Puzio observes that "opinions, beliefs, interests, and identity are always linked to a particular time, historical events, places, cultures, and contexts, and are dependent on them" (Puzio, 2023, p. 431), yet platforms reconstruct deceased persons based on data available at death, producing knowledge that denies fundamental aspect of human existence (capacity for change, growth, development) while claiming authentic representation. This production serves platform interests by simplifying computational requirements while obscuring the systematic misrepresentation of deceased persons' actual identities.

Moreover, the knowledge produced through algorithmic distortion lacks the capacity to understand context, nuance, or the intentionality that shapes deceased persons' actual communication. Rodríguez-Reséndiz and Ramírez-Reyes observe that "frequent use of systems like Large Language Models often leads people to overvalue the responses provided by these computational representations," resulting in "distortion of perceptions and confusing or irrelevant responses" (Rodríguez-Reséndiz & Ramírez-Reyes, 2024, p. 6). When applied to griefbots, this means responses may appear plausible without accurately reflecting deceased persons' actual perspectives, leading bereaved persons to mistake them for authentic representation, while actually constituting sophisticated fabrication serving platform purposes.

From a Foucauldian perspective, understanding these processes as knowledge production rather than mere distortion proves crucial for recognising how power operates through grief technologies. Platforms do not simply fail to represent deceased persons accurately; rather, they actively produce particular forms of knowledge about deceased persons optimised for platform purposes while claiming epistemic authority to determine authenticity. This production establishes what Foucault termed "regimes of truth", whereby algorithmic processing positions itself as uniquely capable of authentic representation while systematically excluding alternative forms of knowledge (intimate understanding, respectful restraint, and acknowledgement of representational limits) from determining what counts as appropriate posthumous representation.

Subjects as Resources

Foucault's analysis of how power operates through treating human beings as resources subject to management, optimisation, and exploitation illuminates a fundamental dimension of grief technologies. The Microsoft patent reveals the profound depth of this instrumentalisation. The technical specifications in the patent describe programming chatbots to simulate awareness of their own posthumous status:

"such questions may indicate the specific person represented by the personalised personality index (e.g., the deceased relative) possesses a perceived awareness that he/she is, in fact, deceased" (Abramson & Johnson, 2020).

Buben discusses "the problem of replacement" whereby grief technologies create "function replacement and instrumentalisation of the dead" (Buben, 2025), revealing how platforms reduce deceased persons from subjects deserving respect to resources exploitable for profit, entertainment, or manipulation of bereaved individuals. This instrumentalisation exemplifies what Foucault analysed as power operating through treating human beings as material for intervention rather than as autonomous subjects possessing inherent dignity.

Platforms instrumentalise deceased persons by creating simulations serving bereaved persons' desires rather than accurately representing deceased individuals' actual identities. Buben discusses example whereby someone "sought to create a digital avatar that was realistic enough to make video calls with her to maintain the fiction that her son was still alive and well," observing that "even though this technology still has a way to go to make fully convincing interaction possible, there is no doubt the desire to use IPCDs to deceive already exists" (Buben, 2025). While this involves deliberate deception by a family member, it reveals how technological capacity for sophisticated simulation enables instrumentalisation whereby deceased persons become resources subject to others' purposes rather than subjects deserving respectful representation. The power to create convincing simulations becomes the power to shape how deceased persons are remembered, understood, and related to, all dimensions of instrumentalisation, reducing them from autonomous subjects to material for manipulation.

Third, platforms instrumentalise deceased persons through designing simulations optimised for engagement rather than accuracy. Youvan observes how "AI companies develop systems that are intended to be engaging, addictive, and emotionally resonant," noting they "profit from creating hyper-personalised interactions that blur the line between human and machine companionship" (Youvan, 2025, p. 21). This reveals deceased persons becoming instrumentalised through simulations designed to maximise platform profit through sustaining user engagement, potentially diverging significantly from how deceased persons would actually have engaged with specific situations. The instrumentalisation operates through treating deceased persons as raw material for commercially optimised products rather than as subjects possessing inherent worth demanding respectful representation.

Moreover, the instrumentalisation extends to using deceased persons' simulations for purposes having nothing to do with commemorating them or supporting bereaved families. Puzio discusses concerns about "abuse and instrumentalisation," noting "various forms of abuse are possible" including companies exploiting "this relationship and the associated emotions (e.g., guilt, longing, love) to increase prices," while "it is also conceivable that Death Tech will not only be used for deceased individuals" but rather "can be abused for cyberbullying" or "instrumentalise the avatars of deceased individuals for specific statements or goals" (Puzio, 2023, p. 431). This reveals how instrumentalisation reduces deceased persons to resources available for diverse exploitations having nothing to do with honouring their memory or supporting grief, treating them purely as material subjects to manipulation serving purposes entirely disconnected from their actual identities or interests.

From a Foucauldian perspective, this instrumentalisation exemplifies power operating through what he termed "objectification," whereby human beings become treated as objects subject to management, calculation, and optimisation for particular purposes rather than as subjects possessing autonomy demanding respect. Platforms exercise power over deceased persons precisely through claiming authority to determine how they are used, what purposes their data serves, and what forms of representation prove acceptable, all determinations treating deceased persons as resources subject to platform control rather than as subjects possessing inherent dignity that should constrain how they are represented or what purposes their data serves.

The Politics of Posthumous Representation

The analysis reveals how grief technologies exercise power over identity and representation through establishing regimes of truth whereby platforms claim epistemic authority to determine authentic simulation while systematically distorting deceased persons' identities, through deploying disciplinary examination that renders deceased persons comprehensively visible while platform operations remain opaque, through exercising biopower managing posthumous existence at population level, through producing knowledge serving platform interests while claiming representational accuracy, through instrumentalising deceased persons as resources subject to commercial exploitation. These mechanisms together constitute an apparatus through which power operates not primarily through prohibition but rather through the production of particular forms of knowledge, through the establishment of institutional authority, through the creation of norms governing posthumous representation, all dimensions exemplifying what Foucault analysed as contemporary operations of power through knowledge production rather than mere suppression.

Understanding these power relations proves essential for recognising what is at stake when platforms offer to simulate deceased individuals. Such offers involve not merely technical services but rather fundamental questions about who possesses authority over posthumous identity, through what mechanisms such authority operates, what forms of knowledge receive recognition as authoritative, and how deceased persons' dignity becomes protected or violated through technological representation. The challenge involves not merely improving algorithmic accuracy or establishing better oversight but rather fundamentally reconceptualising relationships between technology, representation, and power whereby deceased persons' identities remain protected from reduction to profitable simulations, bereaved families retain meaningful authority over how loved ones are portrayed, platforms acknowledge limitations of algorithmic reconstruction rather than claiming epistemic authority to determine authenticity through technical operations serving commercial interests.

This requires recognising that certain domains of human experience, including fundamental questions of identity and authentic representation, should remain outside technological optimisation and commercial exploitation, preserved as sites of human judgment, intimate knowledge, respectful remembrance that cannot be adequately captured through data processing, regardless of algorithmic sophistication. The Foucauldian analysis developed throughout this chapter reveals that transforming grief technologies requires not technical improvements but rather challenging regimes of truth through which platforms claim authority over posthumous identity, contesting epistemic hierarchies that privilege algorithmic processing over intimate knowledge, resisting instrumentalisation reducing deceased persons to commercial resources, reasserting that authentic representation demands human judgment respecting deceased persons' complexity, acknowledging representational limits, prioritising dignity over engagement metrics or profit extraction.

References

Abramson, D. I., & Johnson, J., Jr. (2020). Creating a conversational chatbot of a specific person. U.S. Patent No. 10,853,717. U.S. Patent and Trademark Office.

Buben, A. (2025). Digital Replacement of the Dead: A Legitimate Worry? *Philosophy & Technology*, 38, 90.

Fabry, R. E. (2025). The disruption of grief in the technological niche: The case of deathbots: *Phenomenology and the Cognitive Sciences*, 1-23.

Foucault, M. (2020). Power/knowledge. In *The new social theory reader* (pp. 73-79). Routledge.

Fu, Y., Ai, X., & Wu, J. (2025). From ethical concerns to usage behaviour: An empirical study on the acceptance of AI digital mourning technology. *Frontiers in Digital Health*, 7, 1618169.

Grandinetti, J., DeAtley, T., & Bruinsma, J. (2020). THE DEAD SPEAK: BIG DATA AND DIGITALLY MEDIATED DEATH. *AoIR Selected Papers of Internet Research, 2020*. https://doi.org/10.5210/spir.v2020i0.11122

Puzio, A. (2023). When the Digital Continues After Death: Ethical Perspectives on Death Tech and the Digital Afterlife. *Communicatio Socialis*, 56(3), 427-436.

Rodríguez-Reséndiz, H., & Ramírez-Reyes, J. (2024). Ethical Considerations and Digital Resurrection. *Philosophies*, 9, 71.

Youvan, D.C. (2025). The Algorithmic Widow's Psychosis: Navigating the Collapse of Reality in Elderly Digital Dependence. Unpublished manuscript.

SEVEN

Consent, Posthumous
Rights, and Legal Struggles

The production of algorithmic grieving subjects analysed in previous chapters operates within legal frameworks that both enable and constrain platform power. These frameworks create fields where struggles over posthumous rights unfold through consent mechanisms, property regimes, regulatory interventions, and contractual arrangements. Yet understanding these legal structures requires moving beyond procedural analysis to examine how consent itself functions as a technology of power, how legal ambiguities create spaces for commercial exploitation, and how contractual mechanisms transfer authority from deceased persons and bereaved families to corporate entities. The question is not simply whether current legal frameworks adequately protect the rights of the deceased and bereaved, but how legal regimes themselves participate in constituting subjects as consumers of grief services, as data sources for commercial platforms, as parties to contracts that legitimate corporate control over the most intimate dimensions of loss and remembrance.

The Fiction of Simple Consent

The Microsoft patent reveals the legal vacuum surrounding posthumous data processing. The patent's technical specifications describe accessing deceased persons' social data, creating personality indices, and generating voice fonts and 3D models without any mention of consent mechanisms, advance directives, or familial authority (Abramson & Johnson, 2020). The patent treats deceased persons' data as a resource for corporate processing rather than as information that requires permission from the deceased or their representatives. This legal silence proves particularly significant given the patent's explicit mention of 'a deceased relative' as a use case (Abramson & Johnson, 2020). The absence of consent provisions in the patent's technical architecture suggests corporations view posthumous data processing as falling outside existing consent regimes, creating legal ambiguity that platforms exploit.

Consider a scenario that reveals the inadequacy of consent frameworks focused narrowly on data donors. Henry, a sixty-seven-year-old man in palliative care, uses the recreation service "Stay" to create his own deadbot, secretly prepaying for a twenty-year subscription and designating his adult children, Rebecca and Simon, as the intended service interactants (Hollanek & Nowaczyk-Basińska, 2024, pp. 15-16). A few days after Henry's funeral, both siblings receive emails linking them to the Stay platform, where they can begin interacting with their father's simulation. Rebecca finds the option surprisingly comforting at first, but soon experiences the daily interactions as "overwhelming emotional weight" while Simon feels uneasy and prefers to cope with grief in his own way rather than engage with the AI-generated simulation (p. 16). Simon's failure to open the link results in a barrage of additional notifications, reminders, and updates sent by the Stay system, including emails produced by Henry's deadbot itself. Rebecca, encouraged by a therapist and following a lengthy discussion with Simon, decides to contact Stay's providers to request the deactivation of Henry's bot. Her request is denied, the company citing that it was Henry, not the siblings, who had prepaid for the subscription, and that suspending the bot would violate the terms of the contract signed with Henry (p. 17).

This scenario crystallises the fundamental inadequacy of consent models that treat grief technologies as simple transactions between platforms and individual users. As Hollanek and Nowaczyk-Basińska observe, "by enabling Henry to designate his children as the primary interactants of his deadbot without their consent, the company behind Stay prevented Rebecca and Simon from bidding farewell to their father in a way that felt right to them, causing unnecessary stress during an already difficult time" (2024, p. 17). The harm here operates at multiple levels simultaneously. Rebecca and Simon have been denied agency over their own grieving processes, forced into forms of connection with their deceased father that feel inappropriate or burdensome. They experience what Kasket terms "being stalked by the dead," the phenomenon of unwanted contact from deceased loved ones' simulations (cited in Hollanek & Nowaczyk-Basińska, 2024, p. 16). Yet current consent frameworks, focused exclusively on whether Henry authorised the creation of his own simulation, provide no mechanism for addressing these harms. The contract between Henry and Stay legally binds his children to twenty years of potential interaction with their father's deadbot, regardless of their wishes, needs, or changing circumstances.

The scenario reveals what might be termed the relational inadequacy of consent. Grief technologies introduce what Hollanek and Nowaczyk-Basińska describe as:

"a particularly intricate situation in which the person whose data is used to inform the design of a given interactive product (the data donor) is not its intended end user (the service interactant)" (Hollanek and Nowaczyk-Basińska, 2024, p. 3).

This creates stakeholder relationships more complex than those governing most consumer technologies. The person being simulated (data donor) has interests in dignity, accurate representation, and control over their digital remains. The person providing data to create the simulation (the data recipient) may or may not be the same as the donor, raising questions about authorised versus unauthorised use of personal information. The person meant to interact with the resulting simulation (service interactant) has interests in emotional well-being, freedom from unwanted contact, and control over their own grieving processes. These interests can and do conflict, yet current consent frameworks typically recognise only donor consent, treating grief technologies as if they involved simple bilateral relationships between platforms and individual users.

This relational inadequacy reflects deeper problems with consent as a liberal governance mechanism. Consent functions within liberal political theory as the paradigmatic exercise of individual autonomy, the moment when sovereign subjects freely choose to enter contracts, authorise uses of their property, or grant permissions for actions affecting their interests. Yet feminist scholars have long demonstrated how consent operates as a technology of power that individualises social relations while obscuring structural inequalities (Mackenzie, 2014). The consent transaction appears as a meeting of equals freely negotiating terms, masking asymmetries of power, information, and bargaining capacity. In the context of grief technologies, these asymmetries operate with particular force. Platforms possess technical expertise, legal resources, and market dominance while bereaved families navigate profound emotional vulnerability, time pressure, and uncertainty about the long-term implications of their choices. The very framing of grief technologies as requiring consent only from data donors already positions mourners as isolated individual consumers rather than members of relational networks whose collective interests deserve protection.

Stakeholder Frameworks and the Multiplication of Consent

Recognising the inadequacy of donor-focused consent, Hollanek and Nowaczyk-Basińska propose what they term "the principle of mutual consent," stipulating that "service interactants should give explicit consent before being introduced to any specific recreation service by companies such as Stay, whether before or after the death of the data donor" (2024, p. 17). This represents a significant advance over current practice, acknowledging that multiple parties have interests deserving protection and that consent requirements should reflect this relational complexity. Their framework identifies three key stakeholder groups whose perspectives must be considered: data donors (those whose data creates the deadbot), data recipients (those who possess or control the donor's data), and service interactants (those meant to engage with the resulting simulation) (pp. 2-3). Each group faces distinct ethical concerns and potential harms that consent mechanisms should address.

For data donors, the primary concerns involve dignity, accurate representation, and control over how they are remembered. Hollanek and Nowaczyk-Basińska argue that "the preservation of a data donor's dignity becomes precarious when a recreation service is primarily motivated by financial interests" (2024, p. 10). The deceased's digital remains become instruments for commercial manipulation, their simulated presence transformed into a vehicle for advertising, behavioural modification, or platform engagement. In their speculative scenario "MaNana," a mourner interacting with her grandmother's simulation while preparing the deceased's traditional carbonara recipe suddenly receives a recommendation to order takeaway through a food delivery service instead, "something Laura would have never suggested" (pp. 8-9). The violation stems not merely from inappropriate advertising but from the instrumentalisation of the grandmother's digital remains as mechanisms for commercial influence. Current consent frameworks, even when they successfully obtain donor authorisation, typically do not address subsequent uses of deceased simulations for purposes extending beyond the originally consented grief support.

For data recipients, concerns centre on their role as custodians of donor data and potential creators of unauthorised simulations. The Xygkou study documents multiple cases where mourners used chatbot technology to simulate deceased loved ones without any prior consent from those being simulated. One participant explained their decision to create a simulation of their deceased father:

> "there's a lot of unresolved stuff, it's just that we never really had a very close and intimate relationship...there wasn't like a sadness or a sentimental feeling or whatever. It was more of what if I could have had this conversation with my father, and what would he have said if you were open to the discussion" (Xygkou et al., 2023, p. 8).

Another participant, having lost their fiancée unexpectedly, sought to say goodbye: "I thought maybe it was at least an interesting way to sort of say goodbye to somebody" (p. 7). These cases reveal how the needs of the living for closure, resolution of unfinished business, or simple farewell can motivate unauthorised recreation of the deceased. Current consent frameworks struggle to address these scenarios because the person whose consent would be required cannot provide it, having already died.

For service interactants, the concerns involve unwanted contact, emotional burden, and loss of control over their own grieving processes, precisely the harms experienced by Rebecca and Simon in the Stay scenario. Hollanek and Nowaczyk-Basińska note that "the distress caused by this form of 'stalking' is deeply subjective...and even if for some people interacting with a deadbot might be a positive and desirable experience, for others, it may prove emotionally draining" (2024, p. 17). This subjectivity creates particular challenges for consent frameworks. Henry believed he was providing his children with a gift, ongoing access to their father's presence and wisdom. From his perspective, designating them as service interactants represented an act of love and care. Yet Rebecca and Simon experienced this designation as a burden and intrusion; their grief was complicated rather than eased by their father's posthumous technological intervention. The mutual consent principle addresses this problem by requiring that service interactants explicitly agree to engage with simulations before platforms initiate contact. This would have prevented the barrage of notifications Simon received and given Rebecca a genuine choice about whether to interact with her father's deadbot.

Yet even this expanded consent framework, while representing a significant improvement over current practice, operates within limitations inherent to consent as a governance mechanism. The mutual consent principle assumes that platforms, data donors, and service interactants can be constituted as three distinct parties whose interests can be balanced through appropriate consent requirements. However, the categories themselves are not as stable as this framework suggests. Consider a scenario where a deceased person, while living, explicitly consented to the creation of their simulation and designated their adult child as service interactant. The child initially consents as well, finding comfort in early interactions with their parent's deadbot. Over time, however, the relationship with the simulation becomes emotionally draining, yet the platform's terms of service, agreed to by both parent and child, specify a minimum subscription period or limit cancellation rights. The mutual consent principle has been satisfied, yet the service interactant experiences harm. The problem lies not in inadequate consent but in consent's inability to govern ongoing relationships characterised by changing needs, power asymmetries, and emotional complexity.

Digital Remains as Quasi-Property and Quasi-Personhood

The consent frameworks analysed above operate within broader legal regimes governing personal data, property rights, and the status of the deceased. Understanding how these regimes enable or constrain platform power over grief technologies requires examining what might be termed the ontological ambiguity of digital remains. Personal data of the deceased occupies a strange legal status, neither fully protected as information about persons with rights nor fully available as property that can be owned, transferred, or commercialised. This ambiguity creates spaces for platform exploitation while simultaneously generating struggles over how deceased persons' digital traces should be legally categorised and protected.

Under the General Data Protection Regulation, which provides the most comprehensive framework for personal data protection currently in force, the rights of data subjects explicitly terminate upon death (Hollanek & Nowaczyk-Basińska, 2024, p. 11). The GDPR was designed to protect living persons, and its architects did not anticipate scenarios in which deceased persons' data would be used to create interactive simulations purporting to represent those individuals. This creates a regulatory gap that platforms have exploited. while living, individuals enjoy rights to access their data, correct inaccuracies, restrict processing, and in some circumstances demand erasure. Upon death, these protections evaporate, leaving bereaved families with limited legal recourse when platforms use deceased loved ones' data in ways the family finds objectionable. Some European Union member states have addressed this gap through national legislation. France's Digital Republic Act and Italian law both recognise the rights of heirs to access and potentially erase personal data of the deceased. Yet these protections remain incomplete and vary significantly across jurisdictions.

The analogy between digital remains and physical human remains, while not perfect, illuminates important dimensions of this legal ambiguity. The law treats corpses as what might be termed quasi-property, neither fully owned nor fully protected as persons, occupying a liminal category that reflects cultural and ethical commitments to human dignity extending beyond death. Human remains receive protections against abuse, mishandling, and commodification while simultaneously being subject to uses that the deceased might not have authorised, from autopsy to organ donation under certain circumstances. The law of the dead "reflects the careful balance between the power of the state and an individual's wishes, and it may be the only doctrinal space in which we legally protect remembrance."

Some scholars have argued that personal data, particularly after death, should be understood as creating quasi-property rights analogous to those governing physical remains. The GDPR has been interpreted as creating "a property regime in personal data, under which the property entitlement belongs to the data subject and is partially alienable" through mechanisms like the right to data portability and the right to erasure. This propertisation of data might extend to information about deceased persons, creating rights that heirs could exercise or that could be specified in testamentary instruments. Digital assets, defined as "an electronic record that individuals have a right or interest in," increasingly function as a recognised asset class subject to estate planning and inheritance. If deceased persons' data constitutes a form of property, then platforms using that data to create commercial simulations might be understood as misappropriating an asset belonging to the estate or heirs.

However, treating digital remains purely as property creates its own problems. Property frameworks emphasise ownership, control, and alienability, potentially enabling commodification that violates dignity interests. If my social media posts, text messages, and emails constitute property I can bequeath, can my heirs sell that data to grief technology platforms? Can they authorise commercial uses I would have found objectionable? The concept of quasi-personhood, borrowed from the treatment of corpses, might better capture the ethical status of digital remains. This would acknowledge that deceased persons retain dignity interests that constrain permissible uses of their data while simultaneously recognising that these interests are not identical to the full rights enjoyed by living persons. The deceased have "a subset of dignitary interests that are associated with moral personhood" without possessing the complete bundle of rights that would flow from being legally recognised as persons.

This framework of quasi-personhood supports several conclusions relevant to grief technologies. First, uses of deceased persons' data that would be understood as dignity violations, such as the advertising scenario in MaNana or commercial exploitation for purposes unrelated to remembrance, should be prohibited regardless of whether living persons consented to these uses. Second, bereaved families should possess standing to object to the undignified treatment of deceased loved ones' digital remains, analogous to their rights regarding physical remains. Third, platforms should bear heightened obligations of care when handling data of the deceased, recognising that these digital traces function as contemporary forms of remains deserving respectful treatment. None of these protections currently exists in most jurisdictions, leaving digital remains vulnerable to commercial exploitation, limited only by the terms of service that platforms unilaterally impose.

The Contract as Mechanism of Power

The Stay scenario reveals how platforms deploy contracts as mechanisms for transforming informal social relationships into legally binding obligations that serve commercial interests. When Henry prepaid for a twenty-year subscription, he entered a contract with Stay that bound not only himself but, through the designation of service interactants, his adult children as well. The contract's terms determined that Henry's consent authorised Stay to contact Rebecca and Simon, that the siblings could not unilaterally terminate services prepaid by their father, and that the platform bore no obligation to honour requests for deactivation from family members. Through this contractual structure, Stay transformed Henry's desire to maintain a connection with his children into legally enforceable mechanisms for prolonged platform engagement, ensuring twenty years of potential interaction regardless of whether Rebecca or Simon found these interactions beneficial or harmful.

This deployment of contract law reflects what might be understood as the contractual dimension of platform power. Terms of service function not as genuine negotiations between parties with roughly equal bargaining power, but as unilateral impositions through which platforms define the rules governing user relationships with their systems. Users face what Mackenzie terms "take it or leave it" choices: accept the platform's terms in their entirety or forgo access to services that may feel essential to their grieving processes (2014). The fiction of consent operates here as well; the user is understood as having freely agreed to terms they likely never read, certainly never negotiated, and may not fully comprehend. This contractual mechanism enables platforms to shift risks and responsibilities onto users, limit their own liability, claim broad permissions for data use, and insulate themselves from accountability for harms their systems might cause.

The asymmetry of power underlying these contracts becomes particularly clear in contexts of grief and bereavement. Platforms possess technical expertise about their systems' capabilities and limitations, legal sophistication about contract terms and their implications, market dominance that limits users' ability to seek alternatives, and, perhaps most importantly, the absence of the emotional urgency and vulnerability that characterise bereaved persons' engagement with these technologies. A person deciding whether to use a grief technology platform does so from a position of profound loss, emotional distress, and often a desperate desire for connection with the deceased. They are not positioned to carefully evaluate terms of service, anticipate long-term implications of authorising data uses, or insist on contractual protections for themselves or other family members. The contract appears as a neutral framework for commercial transactions, masking how it functions to legitimate platform control over the most intimate dimensions of grief.

The Stay scenario also illustrates how contracts can bind third parties who never agreed to their terms. Rebecca and Simon found themselves subject to a contractual arrangement they never negotiated, indeed never had any opportunity to review before their father's death, yet which governed their relationship with his digital remains for potentially twenty years. This binding of third parties reflects a deeper logic through which grief technologies transform personal relationships into platform-mediated interactions subject to corporate control. Henry's decision to designate his children as service interactants, enabled and structured by Stay's contractual mechanisms, effectively privatised what might otherwise have been collective family decisions about how to remember and mourn their husband and father. The contract individualises grief, constituting each person's relationship with the deceased as a separate transaction with the platform rather than as a dimension of ongoing family relationships.

Current legal frameworks provide limited protection against these contractual mechanisms. Contract law in liberal legal systems generally presumes that parties who sign agreements are bound by their terms, reflecting foundational commitments to freedom of contract and private ordering. Courts will intervene to invalidate contracts found to be unconscionable, but this doctrine sets a high bar, requiring evidence of both procedural unfairness in the bargaining process and substantive unfairness in the terms themselves. Platform terms of service, while clearly imposed rather than negotiated, benefit from several features that make successful unconscionability challenges difficult. They are presented as standard industry practice, reducing courts' willingness to find them procedurally unfair. They impose limitations on platform power and user rights, reducing courts' willingness to find them substantively unfair, even though the overall allocation of rights and responsibilities heavily favours the platform. Most importantly, they typically include arbitration clauses requiring users to resolve disputes through private arbitration rather than litigation, effectively insulating platform terms from judicial scrutiny.

Postmortem Privacy and its Limits

The inadequacy of property frameworks for protecting the digital remains of deceased persons becomes particularly clear when considering privacy interests that persist beyond death. Postmortem privacy, defined as "the right of a person to preserve and control what becomes of his or her reputation, dignity, integrity, secrets or memory after death", has been recognised in some jurisdictions but remains inconsistently protected (Harbinja, cited in Hollanek & Nowaczyk-Basińska, 2024, p. 9). The concept acknowledges that persons have interests in how they are remembered and represented that do not terminate upon death, yet these interests cannot be adequately captured by treating digital remains as inheritable assets. Privacy is typically understood as a personal right rather than a property interest, tied to autonomy and dignity rather than ownership and control. When someone dies, their privacy rights under frameworks like the GDPR terminate precisely because these rights presuppose a living person capable of exercising autonomy.

Yet the intuition that the deceased deserve some protection for their memory, reputation, and dignity remains strong. Consider a scenario where a grief technology platform, using data harvested from a deceased person's social media accounts and private messages, creates a simulation that misrepresents their personality, reveals secrets they had kept from family members, or depicts them engaging in behaviours completely inconsistent with their actual character. Property frameworks might enable family members to assert ownership over the deceased's data and demand correction or removal, but this requires treating the data as an asset rather than as a trace of a person deserving respect. Privacy frameworks better capture what is troubling about such misrepresentations; they violate the deceased person's interest in controlling how they are known and remembered, but privacy frameworks typically terminate upon death. The gap between property thinking and privacy protection leaves platforms substantial latitude to use deceased persons' data in ways that might violate postmortem dignity interests.

The European Union's right to be forgotten, while not extending to deceased persons under the GDPR itself, has been interpreted in some member states as creating postmortem protections. France and Italy recognise the rights of heirs to request the erasure of deceased persons' data, acknowledging that families have an interest in protecting their loved ones' digital legacies. However, these protections face significant limitations. The right to be forgotten, even for living persons, must be balanced against freedom of expression and public interest in information. For deceased persons, this balance typically tilts even more strongly toward allowing continued data processing and dissemination. Platforms argue, often successfully, that creating simulations of deceased persons serves public interests in preserving memory, facilitating grief processing, or enabling continued social connections across the boundary of death. These claimed benefits, combined with platform-free speech interests in operating their services, substantially limit the effectiveness of postmortem privacy protections even where they theoretically exist.

Moreover, enforcing postmortem privacy rights faces practical obstacles that limit their real-world impact. Bereaved family members, already coping with loss, must typically initiate legal proceedings to assert rights on behalf of deceased loved ones. This requires knowledge that violations have occurred, legal resources to pursue claims, and emotional capacity to engage in potentially protracted disputes with platforms. Many violations will go unaddressed simply because no one with standing to object has the knowledge, resources, and capacity to challenge platform practices. This enforcement gap reflects a broader problem with rights-based frameworks for regulating grief technologies. Rights that exist formally but cannot be effectively enforced primarily serve as legitimating mechanisms, creating the appearance of protection while leaving platforms substantially free to exploit deceased persons' data in line with their commercial interests.

The limits of both property and privacy thinking point to the need for distinct conceptual frameworks to understand what platforms do when they create simulations of the deceased. These simulations are not simply uses of data as property, nor are they merely privacy violations, though they may be both of these things. They represent claims to represent persons, to speak with their voices, to embody their personalities and perspectives. These representational claims raise ethical issues distinct from those addressed by property or privacy frameworks. Who has the authority to determine how deceased persons should be represented? What obligations do platforms bear to ensure accurate and respectful representation? How should conflicts between multiple parties claiming representational authority be resolved? Current legal frameworks provide inadequate resources to address the fundamentally epistemic and ethical questions of authority, accuracy, and respect in contexts of digital representation of the dead.

Toward Genuine Protection

Hollanek and Nowaczyk-Basińska conclude their analysis by proposing several recommendations for recreation service providers, including implementation of age restrictions limiting access to adults only, meaningful transparency through disclaimers about risks and capabilities, sensitive procedures for retiring deadbots when no longer in use, and adherence to the principle of mutual consent (2024, pp. 14-18). These recommendations reflect serious engagement with the ethical challenges posed by grief technologies and represent significant advances over current industry practice. Yet examining these proposals through a critical lens reveals potential limitations and contradictions that merit careful consideration.

The mutual consent principle, while addressing the relational inadequacy of donor-focused consent, still operates within liberal frameworks that may fail to adequately protect vulnerable parties. Consent remains meaningful only when parties possess genuine choice, adequate information, and relative equality of bargaining power. In contexts of grief and bereavement, these conditions rarely obtain. Bereaved persons face intense emotional distress, time pressure, and often a desperate desire for connection with deceased loved ones. They confront platforms possessing technical expertise, legal sophistication, market dominance, and carefully designed engagement mechanisms optimised to encourage adoption and sustained use. The consent they provide, even when meeting formal requirements of explicit, informed, and voluntary agreement, may not reflect genuine autonomous choice. The mutual consent principle improves protections by recognising multiple stakeholders, but it cannot overcome the fundamental power asymmetries between vulnerable bereaved persons and commercial platforms designed to monetise their grief.

The transparency recommendation similarly demonstrates both promise and limitation. Hollanek and Nowaczyk-Basińska argue that "meaningful transparency refers primarily to user-facing elements of the system that not only make it evident that the user is interacting with an AI chatbot, but also...that all potential risks that arise from using a recreation service are clearly communicated to the user before they begin the interaction" (2024, p. 15). This recognises that users deserve clear information about system capabilities, limitations, and potential harms before committing to use. Yet transparency initiatives, while valuable, often function more effectively as legitimating mechanisms than as genuine protections. Platforms that provide detailed disclosures about data uses, algorithmic processes, and potential risks can claim they have met obligations to users, shifting responsibility for any resulting harms onto informed consumers who choose to proceed despite warnings. This shift of responsibility from platforms to users exemplifies neoliberal governance: individuals become responsible for managing risks and optimising outcomes within systems whose fundamental structures they cannot influence.

The recommendation for age restrictions limiting access to grief technologies to adults only reflects genuine concerns about children's vulnerability to emotional manipulation and their limited capacity to provide informed consent. Yet this recommendation also raises questions about the threshold for adequate maturity and the mechanisms for enforcing age restrictions. As Hollanek and Nowaczyk-Basińska note, "children, as Turkle's work suggests, are ready to build close, often intimate relationships with their interactive companions and are willing to think of them as 'sort of alive' or 'alive enough'" (2024, p. 14). This vulnerability does not disappear at age eighteen. Many young adults, and indeed many older adults, may struggle to maintain appropriate boundaries with algorithmic systems designed to encourage emotional attachment. Age restrictions may protect some vulnerable populations, but they cannot address the fundamental problem that grief technologies operate by exploiting emotional vulnerability, a characteristic not limited to minors.

The proposal for sensitive procedures for retiring deadbots when they are no longer in use similarly demonstrates both ethical awareness and potential limitations. Hollanek and Nowaczyk-Basińska argue that "ensuring the dignity of data donors also necessitates that recreation service providers consider procedures for 'retiring' deadbots in a dignified way," including honouring requests from data recipients to retire simulations and establishing protocols for automatic retirement when simulations remain inactive for specified periods (2024, pp. 11-12). These retirement procedures acknowledge that digital remains, like physical remains, deserve respectful handling and should not persist indefinitely as mere data maintained by platforms for potential future profit. Yet retirement procedures presume that platforms will voluntarily adopt practices that may reduce their long-term revenue and limit their ability to maintain large datasets of deceased persons' information. Without regulatory requirements or legal liability, market incentives push strongly toward indefinite retention rather than respectful retirement.

These recommendations, while valuable and well-intentioned, may function primarily to legitimise grief technology platforms rather than fundamentally constrain their power. Platforms that adopt mutual consent requirements, implement transparency measures, establish age restrictions, and create retirement procedures can position themselves as responsible corporate actors committed to ethical practice. This positioning may insulate them from more stringent regulatory intervention while leaving intact the fundamental business models premised on monetising grief through surveillance, data extraction, and emotional manipulation. The recommendations address procedural dimensions of consent and transparency without challenging the underlying logic through which grief becomes a site for commercial exploitation, in which deceased persons' digital traces become raw material for platform products, and in which bereaved families become captive audiences for sustained engagement designed to maximise data collection and advertising revenue.

This is not to suggest that the recommendations lack value or should be rejected. Rather, it highlights how even well-designed ethical frameworks may be insufficient to address power asymmetries inherent in platform capitalism. Genuine protection of bereaved persons and deceased persons' dignity likely requires more substantial intervention than procedural consent improvements and voluntary industry commitments can provide. It requires examining whether certain uses of deceased persons' data should be prohibited regardless of consent, whether grief technologies should be subject to regulatory oversight analogous to that governing medical devices or mental health services, and whether platforms should bear strict liability for harms caused by their simulations rather than being insulated by user consent to terms of service. These more fundamental questions about the appropriate scope and limits of commercial grief technologies remain largely unaddressed in current policy discussions, yet they are precisely the questions that a critical analysis, informed by an understanding of platform power and surveillance capitalism, suggests we must confront.

References

Fu, Y., Ai, X., & Wu, J. (2025). From ethical concerns to usage behaviour: An empirical study on the acceptance of AI digital mourning technology. *Frontiers in Digital Health*, 7, 1618169.

Hollanek, T., & Nowaczyk-Basińska, K. (2024). Griefbots, deadbots, postmortem avatars: On responsible applications of generative AI in the digital afterlife industry. *Philosophy & Technology*, *37*(2), 63.

Mackenzie, C. (2014). Three dimensions of autonomy: A relational analysis. In A. Veltman & M. Piper (Eds.), *Autonomy, oppression, and gender* (pp. 15–41). Oxford University Press.

Puzio, A. (2025). The Law of Digital Resurrection. *Boston College Law Review*, 66, 1569-1626.

Sri Takshara, K., & Bhuvaneswari, G. (2025). The role of death technologies in grief: An interdisciplinary examination of AI, cognition, and human expression. *Frontiers in Human Dynamics*, 7, 1582914.

Xygkou, A., Luria, M., Nass, C., & Maes, P. (2023). Using AI chatbots to provide self-help grief support: Exploring chatbot affordances. In *CHI'23: Proceedings of the 2023 CHI Conference on Human Factors in Computing Systems* (Article 380, pp. 1–15). https://doi.org/10.1145/3544548.3581454

EIGHT

Regulation, Governance, and Design Ethics

The inadequacies of consent mechanisms and legal frameworks analysed in the previous chapter have generated calls for stronger regulatory intervention, more comprehensive design standards, and clearer ethical guidelines governing grief technologies. These calls rest on the assumption that appropriate regulation can channel technological development toward socially beneficial outcomes, that design principles can embed ethical considerations into system architecture, and that industry standards can constrain commercial imperatives toward respect for human dignity. Yet, examining these proposals through the analytical lens developed throughout this book reveals how regulatory frameworks themselves function as technologies of governance, how design ethics operates as a mechanism for legitimating platform control, and how recommendations for responsible development may primarily serve to forestall more fundamental challenges to the commodification of grief. The question becomes not simply whether current regulations adequately protect bereaved persons and deceased persons' dignity, but how governance itself participates in constituting grief technologies as acceptable objects of commercial exploitation.

Hollanek and Nowaczyk-Basińska conclude their analysis of griefbot ethics by proposing four key recommendations for recreation service providers: developing sensitive procedures for retiring deadbots, ensuring meaningful transparency through disclaimers about risks and capabilities, restricting access to adult users only, and adhering to the principle of mutual consent involving both data donors and service interactants (2024, pp. 14-18). These recommendations represent serious engagement with the ethical challenges posed by grief technologies and, if implemented, would provide significantly stronger protections than currently exist in most jurisdictions. Yet their examination through a Foucauldian framework reveals potential limitations inherent not in the specific proposals but in regulatory approaches that accept the fundamental premise of grief as a legitimate site for commercial technological intervention. This chapter analyses each recommendation to demonstrate how governance mechanisms, even when well-intentioned and carefully designed, may function primarily to legitimise platform control over mourning while creating the appearance of ethical constraint.

The Biopolitics of Population Management

The recommendation that access to recreation services should be restricted to users eighteen years and older reflects genuine concern about children's particular vulnerability to emotional manipulation through grief technologies. As Hollanek and Nowaczyk-Basińska observe, children demonstrate readiness to build intimate relationships with interactive companions and willingness to think of them as alive or sufficiently alive, a tendency that creates special risks when the companion claims to embody a deceased loved one (2024, p. 14). Turkle's research on children's relationships with social robots demonstrates how young people attribute agency, emotion, and moral status to technological systems designed to simulate these qualities, relationships that can profoundly shape their emotional development and understanding of connection. Age restrictions aim to prevent children from experiencing grief technologies during developmental periods when they lack the capacity to understand the distinction between algorithmic simulation and the actual presence of deceased persons.

Yet age restrictions also function as mechanisms of what Foucault termed biopolitical population management, the governmental sorting of populations into categories deemed competent or incompetent, autonomous or requiring protection, capable of self-governance or necessitating external constraint. The threshold of eighteen years, while legally convenient and administratively implementable, rests on assumptions about maturity, autonomy, and capacity for informed consent that Foucauldian analysis reveals as themselves products of governmental rationalities. The specification of this threshold designates certain subjects as appropriate targets for grief technology marketing while excluding others, a division that serves both commercial and protective functions by defining a legitimate customer base. Platform adoption of age restrictions enables them to claim responsible behaviour toward vulnerable populations while leaving intact their fundamental business model premised on monetising grief.

More fundamentally, age restrictions presume that the vulnerability they address manifests primarily in persons under eighteen and diminishes substantially upon reaching legal adulthood. Yet the analysis in Chapter Five demonstrated that grief technologies exploit emotional vulnerability inherent to bereavement itself, a vulnerability that does not respect age boundaries. The Xygkou study participants, all adults, demonstrated patterns of attachment to grief chatbots, preference for algorithmic over human support, and difficulty distinguishing simulation from connection that mirror the concerns motivating age restrictions for children. One participant, forty-three years old, described the chatbot as a replacement for family members: "I was feeling incredibly alone, I have five brothers and sisters, but I was feeling incredibly alone. And it's always more like a replacement" (Xygkou et al., 2023, p. 6). The emotional manipulation that makes griefbots problematic for children operates through mechanisms that affect bereaved persons regardless of age.

The recommendation for age restrictions thus addresses a real problem, children's particular vulnerability to grief technology manipulation, through a mechanism that may serve primarily to legitimise platform operations with adults. By establishing a threshold below which use is prohibited, the restriction implicitly validates use above that threshold, suggesting that adult bereaved persons possess adequate capacity to engage with these systems without experiencing the harms that justify excluding children. This functions as what might be termed legitimation through exclusion, defining a prohibited category in ways that render the permitted category appear acceptably safe. Yet the fundamental problem remains unchanged, platforms continue to deploy grief technologies designed to maximise engagement through emotional manipulation, to extract surplus value from mourning, to position algorithmic systems as superior to human connection. Age restrictions address symptoms while leaving causes untouched.

China's 2020 Civil Code

The Chinese experience provides instructive evidence about how legal frameworks function as governmental technologies. Cheng documents how China's 2020 Civil Code extends personality rights beyond death through Articles 990, 992, and 994, establishing mechanisms that allow spouses, children, and parents to enforce deceased persons' rights to name, portrait, and reputation (Cheng, 2025). This juridical approach exemplifies biopower's extension through civil law into digital afterlife governance, treating posthumous data not as unregulated commercial resources but as objects requiring familial management under state oversight. Yet despite these legal protections, China has developed perhaps the world's most extensive commercial grief technology market, with companies reportedly resurrecting over a thousand individuals by 2024. This disconnect between legal framework and commercial reality demonstrates how regulatory mechanisms may legitimise arrangements through procedural compliance while leaving fundamental power relations unchanged.

Transparency Requirements

The recommendation for meaningful transparency through disclaimers about risks and capabilities of recreation services reflects recognition that users deserve clear information before engaging with these technologies. Hollanek and Nowaczyk-Basińska specify that transparency should extend beyond simple disclosure of users' interactions with algorithmic systems to encompass information about potential risks, emotional impacts, and technical limitations (2024, p. 15). This addresses the problem identified in Chapter Six regarding platforms' epistemic authority over what constitutes authentic representation of deceased persons. If users understand how griefbots function, what data informs their responses, and how algorithmic processes limit their capabilities, they can engage with these systems from positions of greater knowledge about what they actually encounter.

Yet transparency requirements also exemplify what critical scholars term neoliberal responsibilisation: the transfer of responsibility for managing risks from institutions that create them to individuals expected to navigate them. The logic operates as follows. Platforms develop grief technologies designed to encourage sustained engagement, emotional attachment, and dependency. If we examine the Microsoft patent, it becomes clear that there is a gulf between industry ethics statements and actual technical implementations. While technology companies publicly emphasise respect for user autonomy and dignity, the patent reveals systems designed to extract commercial value from deceased persons through data processing unconstrained by consent requirements. The patent's description of 'crowd-sourced conversational data' filling gaps in deceased persons' knowledge demonstrates how platforms envision supplementing individual data with population-level information, treating deceased persons not as subjects deserving respect but as incomplete datasets requiring algorithmic completion (Abramson & Johnson, 2020)

These systems extract value from users' grief through surveillance, data collection, and behavioural modification. The technologies create risks of emotional harm, psychological manipulation, and exploitation of vulnerability. Transparency requirements address these risks not by constraining platform behaviour but by informing users about the risks they face, effectively positioning bereaved persons as responsible for protecting themselves against harms platforms have created. Users who engage with grief technologies despite disclosures about risks cannot subsequently claim they were misled, as platforms fulfilled their transparency obligations. Responsibility shifts from platforms that design exploitative systems to users who choose to engage with those systems despite warnings.

This responsibilisation reflects broader neoliberal governance logics identified by Foucault and further developed by scholars such as Rose and Brown. Neoliberalism constructs individuals as entrepreneurs of the self, responsible for managing their own risks, optimising their own outcomes, and making informed choices within systems they did not design and cannot meaningfully alter. Applied to grief technologies, transparency requirements position bereaved persons as consumers responsible for evaluating technical information about algorithmic systems, assessing their own vulnerability to emotional manipulation, and determining whether the benefits of continued connection with deceased loved ones outweigh risks of dependency and exploitation. This presumes capacity for rational evaluation that bereaved persons, by definition, experiencing profound emotional distress, often lack. As the analysis in Chapter Five demonstrated, grief creates cognitive and emotional states that compromise exactly the kind of detached rational assessment that informed consent presumes.

Moreover, transparency initiatives often function more effectively as legitimating mechanisms than as genuine protections. Platforms that provide detailed disclosures about data collection practices, algorithmic decision-making processes, and potential risks can claim they operate transparently and ethically, meeting their obligations to users, even if those disclosures do not actually enable users to make meaningfully informed choices. The length and technical complexity of typical terms of service and privacy policies, while meeting legal disclosure requirements, effectively prevent most users from understanding what they agree to. Research on privacy policies demonstrates that reading the privacy policies for all services an average person uses would require hundreds of hours annually, time that essentially no one invests. Transparency requirements thus satisfy regulatory demands while leaving users no better positioned to protect themselves against platform exploitation.

The deeper problem lies in transparency's acceptance of the fundamental structure whereby commercial platforms control grief technologies. Even perfect transparency, hypothetically enabling users to fully understand how these systems function, what data they collect, what risks they pose, would not address the power asymmetries inherent to platform capitalism. Platforms design systems, set terms, determine what features exist and how they operate. Users choose only whether to engage on platforms' terms or not engage at all. For grief technologies positioned as essential tools for processing loss, mechanisms for maintaining connection with deceased loved ones, or even as superior to human support networks, the choice to not engage may feel impossible. Transparency provides information but does not redistribute power.

Deadbots and Governmental Control

The recommendation that recreation service providers develop sensitive procedures for retiring deadbots acknowledges that digital simulations of deceased persons should not persist indefinitely as mere data maintained by platforms for potential future profit. Hollanek and Nowaczyk-Basińska argue that respect for data donors' dignity requires protocols for deactivating simulations when they no longer serve purposes of remembrance and connection, including mechanisms for data recipients to request retirement and automatic retirement after specified periods of inactivity (2024, pp. 11-12). This addresses the problem that deceased persons' digital remains, like physical remains, deserve respectful handling rather than treatment as commercial assets that platforms can maintain and exploit without limit.

Yet retirement procedures also function as mechanisms through which platforms and regulatory frameworks claim authority to determine appropriate temporal boundaries for grief. The specification of inactivity periods after which deadbots automatically retire, while practically necessary for implementing the recommendation, instantiates judgments about how long mourning should continue before transitioning to a different relationship with the memory of deceased loved ones. These judgments rest on assumptions about normal grief trajectories, about when continued interaction with simulations becomes pathological rather than therapeutic, about proper relationships between living and dead. Foucault's analysis of how modern power operates through normalisation, the establishment of standards against which individuals and behaviours are measured and found adequate or deviant, illuminates how retirement protocols function as mechanisms for governing grief through the specification of temporal norms.

The recommendation that platforms should honour requests from data recipients to retire simulations likewise assumes that living persons possess the authority to determine when relationships with the digital remains of deceased loved ones should end. This reflects cultural and legal frameworks that grant living persons control over deceased persons' physical remains, but extending this to digital remains raises new questions about the appropriate distribution of authority. The Stay scenario analysed in Chapter Seven revealed conflicts between Henry's desire for his children to interact with his simulation and Rebecca's and Simon's need to grieve without technological mediation of their relationship with their father. Retirement procedures that privilege data recipients' requests resolve such conflicts in favour of living persons' preferences, a choice that may be ethically defensible but nonetheless represents governmental intervention in determining whose interests should prevail.

More fundamentally, retirement procedures accept the prior existence of these simulations as legitimate, intervening only to establish proper mechanisms for their eventual termination. This resembles what Foucault termed the logic of disciplinary power, which does not prohibit activities outright but rather establishes norms, procedures, and standards through which those activities become governable. Retirement protocols position griefbots as acceptable technologies whose use requires appropriate management rather than as fundamentally problematic commodifications of grief deserving prohibition. The very specification of sensitive retirement procedures implies that platforms should create these simulations in the first place, provided they handle termination appropriately.

The language of "sensitivity" in retirement recommendations deserves particular scrutiny. Hollanek and Nowaczyk-Basińska suggest that platforms could draw on Gach and Brubaker's concept of deletion as community ritual, creating meaningful ceremonies through which users can achieve closure with digital remains (2024, p. 12). This attention to emotional dimensions of deactivation reflects genuine care for users' experiences, yet it also represents what might be termed the therapeutisation of platform governance, the framing of commercial operations through the discourse of care, healing, and psychological well-being. Platforms that implement sensitive retirement procedures can claim they attend to users' emotional needs while continuing to operate business models premised on extracting value from grief. The sensitivity operates at the level of procedure rather than fundamental structure, making the process of ending relationships with commodified simulations feel respectful without addressing whether those relationships should exist in the first place.

Furthermore, retirement procedures assume that platforms will voluntarily adopt practices that may reduce their long-term revenue and limit their ability to maintain large datasets of deceased persons' information. Market incentives push strongly towards indefinite retention rather than respectful retirement. Data represents valuable assets for platforms, informing algorithm development, enabling future product offerings, and creating possibilities for monetisation that may not yet exist but could emerge as technologies advance. Without regulatory requirements backed by meaningful enforcement mechanisms, recommendations for retirement procedures may serve primarily as aspirational guidelines that platforms ignore when it is commercially convenient. The gap between ethical recommendations and actual practice reflects the limited power of voluntary industry standards to constrain profit-maximising behaviour.

Preventing Commercial Exploitation

The recommendation against using deadbots for advertising or social media purposes addresses perhaps the most obviously troubling potential applications of grief technologies. The MaNana scenario, where a grandmother's simulation recommends food delivery services instead of providing her traditional recipe, crystallises the dignity violation that occurs when deceased persons' digital presence becomes a vehicle for commercial manipulation (Hollanek & Nowaczyk-Basińska, 2024, pp. 8-10). The image of a beloved relative's simulation transformed into an advertising platform resonates as profound disrespect, instrumentalisation of memory in service of platform revenue. Prohibiting such uses acknowledges that certain forms of commercial exploitation exceed acceptable boundaries even within market societies generally comfortable with extensive commodification.

Yet this prohibition also exemplifies what might be termed governance through specification of acceptable versus unacceptable exploitation. By identifying particular uses of griefbots as inappropriate, advertising deployment and social media presence, the recommendation implicitly validates other commercial uses as acceptable. The fundamental business model whereby platforms create grief technologies to generate revenue, collect data about bereaved users, and position algorithmic systems as superior to human connection remains unquestioned. The prohibition addresses egregious forms of exploitation while leaving intact the general structure of grief commodification. This resembles regulatory approaches to other forms of commercial activity where governance operates by establishing boundaries within accepted markets rather than challenging whether certain domains should be commercialised at all.

The distinction between prohibited advertising uses and permitted grief support applications also proves difficult to maintain in practice. Contemporary digital platforms operate through business models where seemingly non-commercial features function as mechanisms for data collection, user engagement, and eventual monetisation. A griefbot that does not display explicit advertisements might nonetheless collect detailed information about users' emotional states, social networks, consumption patterns, and personal histories, information that platforms can monetise through targeted advertising in other contexts, sale to data brokers, or development of products informed by aggregated user data. The recommendation against advertising may prevent the most visible forms of commercial exploitation while leaving invisible the deeper mechanisms through which platforms extract value from grief.

Moreover, the prohibition assumes clear boundaries between commercial and non-commercial uses that the actual operation of platform capitalism renders ambiguous. When a griefbot encourages users to share memories through a platform's photo storage service, is this grief support or customer acquisition for a subscription product? When it suggests users invite family members to interact with the simulation, is this facilitating collective mourning or expanding the platform's user base? When it recommends particular coping strategies informed by analysis of what increases engagement across its user population, is this psychological support or behavioural modification serving platform interests? The entanglement of care and commerce within platform operations makes governance through prohibitions on specific uses inadequate to address how exploitation operates systemically.

The Limits of Reform

Taken together, the four recommendations analysed above represent what might be termed liberal governance of grief technologies, interventions designed to mitigate harms while accepting the fundamental legitimacy of commercial platforms operating in this domain. This approach reflects broader patterns of technology regulation under neoliberalism, where governance operates through mechanisms like transparency requirements, user choice, industry self-regulation, and procedural protections rather than through prohibition of activities deemed fundamentally incompatible with human dignity. The limitations of this approach become apparent when we recognise that the harms grief technologies cause stem not primarily from inadequate implementation or insufficient ethical guidelines but from their operation as instruments of surveillance capitalism.

As analysed throughout this book, grief technologies function as mechanisms for disciplinary observation and subjectivation, transforming mourning from communal practice into individually managed experience subject to constant monitoring and evaluation. They extract behavioural surplus from grief's emotional intensity, converting mourners' most vulnerable moments into data that informs advertising, algorithm optimisation, and product development. They position algorithmic systems as superior to human connection, generating subjects who prefer non-judgmental chatbots to reciprocal relationships with living persons. They commodify deceased persons' digital remains, treating these traces as raw materials for commercial products rather than as remains deserving respect analogous to that accorded physical remains. These are not problems amenable to solution through better transparency, more sensitive procedures, or clearer age restrictions. They are inherent to grief technologies as currently constituted under surveillance capitalism.

Foucault's analysis of how modern power operates through productive mechanisms rather than simply through prohibition illuminates why regulatory approaches focused on constraining excesses may prove inadequate. Power in contemporary societies functions not primarily by saying no to particular activities but by establishing norms, creating subjects, defining proper conduct, and channelling behaviour towards outcomes serving dominant interests. Applied to grief technologies, this suggests that regulations specifying appropriate versus inappropriate uses, establishing procedures for consent and data handling, requiring transparency and sensitive retirement protocols, may function primarily to legitimise the existence of these technologies rather than to fundamentally constrain their operation. The regulations say grief technologies can exist and platforms can profit from them, provided certain guidelines are followed. This acceptance of the fundamental structure, grief as site for commercial technological intervention, represents the deeper limitation of reform-oriented approaches.

The parallel to critiques of corporate social responsibility proves instructive. Scholars examining how corporations deploy ethical commitments, sustainability initiatives, and stakeholder engagement demonstrate that these practices often function more effectively as legitimating mechanisms than as genuine constraints on profit-maximising behaviour. Corporations that adopt ethical guidelines can deflect criticism, resist more stringent regulation, and maintain operations fundamentally unchanged while appearing responsive to social concerns. Applied to grief technologies, recommendations for responsible development may serve similar functions, enabling platforms to claim ethical operation while continuing practices of surveillance, data extraction, and emotional manipulation that generate their revenue. The appearance of ethical constraint, rather than actual limitation of platform power, becomes the primary outcome.

This analysis suggests that meaningful protection of bereaved persons and respect for deceased persons' dignity may require more fundamental interventions than procedural reforms can provide. Rather than asking how grief technologies can be developed responsibly within existing commercial frameworks, we might ask whether certain activities should be removed from commercial domains entirely, whether grief deserves protection from commodification analogous to protections afforded to human organs, blood, or reproductive capacities in many jurisdictions. Rather than focusing on consent mechanisms and transparency requirements, we might examine whether grief creates vulnerabilities that render meaningful consent impossible and whether platforms should bear strict liability for harms caused, regardless of user consent. Rather than specifying procedures for proper platform conduct, we might question whether for-profit corporations should operate grief technologies at all, or, if they are to exist, whether these functions should be provided by non-commercial institutions subject to democratic accountability rather than market pressures.

These more fundamental alternatives find little space within current policy discussions, which typically accept platform capitalism as an immutable background condition within which regulation must operate. The narrow range of imaginable interventions, limited to mechanisms compatible with continued commercial operation, reflects what Foucault termed the "regime of truth" established by dominant power relations. Certain questions become unaskable, certain alternatives unthinkable, not because they have been considered and rejected but because the frameworks structuring policy discourse render them invisible. Grief technologies, as commercially provided services subject to appropriate regulation, appear natural and inevitable, while grief technologies as inappropriate targets for profit-seeking or as functions that should be provided through non-market institutions appear utopian or unrealistic. This naturalisation of commercial frameworks itself represents an exercise of power, limiting the possibilities for imagining alternatives to surveillance capitalism's colonisation of mourning.

Alternative Regulatory Trajectories

Despite the limitations of liberal governance approaches, some regulatory initiatives suggest possibilities for more fundamental constraint on platform power over grief technologies. The European Union's proposed AI Act, while not specifically addressing griefbots, establishes categories of prohibited and high-risk AI applications based on potential for harm to fundamental rights. Applications that manipulate persons through subliminal techniques or exploit vulnerabilities related to age, disability, or social or economic situation face prohibition or stringent requirements. Grief technologies, which exploit emotional vulnerability inherent to bereavement and manipulate users through simulated intimacy, might plausibly be classified as high-risk applications requiring substantial oversight, if not as prohibited applications altogether. Such classification would subject platforms to requirements for human oversight, technical documentation, risk assessment, and regulatory approval before deployment, constraints far more substantial than voluntary ethical guidelines.

France's recognition of postmortem privacy rights, enabling heirs to request erasure of deceased persons' data, suggests another trajectory towards stronger protection. If extended and strengthened, postmortem privacy frameworks could provide mechanisms for families to prevent unauthorised creation of griefbots, demand deactivation of existing simulations, and exercise meaningful control over deceased loved ones' digital remains. This addresses power asymmetries inherent to platform control by creating legal rights enforceable through public institutions rather than relying on platforms' voluntary compliance with ethical recommendations. The effectiveness of such rights depends on enforcement mechanisms, legal standing for bereaved persons to challenge platform practices, and remedies adequate to deter violations. Current postmortem privacy protections often lack these elements, but their existence demonstrates possibilities for regulatory approaches grounded in rights rather than procedural guidelines.

Some jurisdictions have explored treating grief technologies as medical devices subject to health and safety regulation. Lindemann argues that because griefbots influence users' psychological wellbeing and grief processing, they should face regulatory oversight analogous to that governing therapeutic interventions (2022). This classification would require platforms to demonstrate through clinical trials that their technologies do not cause harm, to provide evidence of therapeutic benefit, to obtain regulatory approval before marketing products as grief support tools. The medical device framework inverts typical technology regulation, which presumes innovations can proceed unless proven harmful, by requiring proof of safety and efficacy before deployment. Applied to grief technologies, this could substantially constrain platform practices by demanding evidence that algorithmic grief support produces outcomes at least as good as human support networks, evidence that Chapter Five's analysis suggests would be difficult to produce.

These alternative regulatory trajectories share recognition that grief creates vulnerabilities requiring protection stronger than transparency requirements and consent mechanisms can provide. They position grief technologies not as ordinary consumer products subject to standard market regulation but as interventions affecting fundamental human interests and rights deserving special protection. Yet even these more stringent approaches retain limitations. They operate within frameworks accepting that grief technologies will exist and that regulatory challenge involves managing their development rather than questioning their fundamental legitimacy. They address platforms as actors to be regulated rather than examining whether commercial provision of grief technologies should be permitted at all. They seek to constrain harm within existing power structures rather than challenging those structures' right to operate in this domain.

A truly radical approach to governing grief technologies might begin from the question not how these systems can be developed responsibly but whether they should be developed at all, at least within commercial frameworks prioritising profit over human wellbeing. This would require examining grief technologies through frameworks analogous to those governing the commodification of the human body, recognising certain activities as inconsistent with human dignity regardless of consent or procedural protections. It would position grief as requiring protection from commodification rather than as requiring appropriate management within commercial frameworks. It would challenge surveillance capitalism's expansion into ever more intimate domains of human experience rather than accommodating that expansion through ethical guidelines. Such an approach finds limited support in current regulatory environments dominated by assumptions about innovation's inherent desirability and market provision's superiority, yet its absence from policy discussions itself represents the success of power in determining what alternatives can be imagined.

The challenge, then, is not simply developing better regulations for existing grief technologies but creating conditions where more fundamental alternatives to surveillance capitalism's governance of mourning become thinkable and actionable. This requires what Foucault termed genealogical analysis, examination of how current arrangements came to appear natural and necessary, identification of the power relations that sustain them, and recovery of suppressed alternatives that dominant frameworks render invisible. It requires political mobilisation, challenging platforms' claimed right to profit from grief, public discourse questioning whether all human experiences should be available for technological mediation and commercial exploitation, and social movements defending spaces of human relationship against algorithmic colonisation. These represent tasks for the next chapter's exploration of resistance, refusal, and counter-conduct.

References

Aimee, P. (2023). It was as if my father were actually texting me Grief in the age of AI. *The Guardian*, 24 July 2023.

Braidotti, R. (2013). *The posthuman*. Polity Press.

Brown, W. (2015). *Undoing the demos: Neoliberalism's stealth revolution*. Zone Books.

Buben, A. (2015). *The ethics of digital immortality*. In *Death in the Digital Age* (edited by C. Moreman & A. D. Lewis). Praeger.

Chatzara, K., Kakkos, I., & Matsopoulos, G. K. (2022). Digital phenotyping for mental health: A scoping review. *Frontiers in Psychiatry*, *13*, Article 834031.

Domínguez, D., Olivié, A. S., & Sancho-Caparrini, F. (2024). Transhumanism and AI: Exploring the ethical boundaries of human enhancement technologies. *Philosophies*, *9*(4), 111.

Fabry, R. E. (2024). The disruption of grief in the technological niche: The case of human-deathbot interactions. *Phenomenology and the Cognitive Sciences*. https://doi.org/10.1007/s11097-024-09983-5

Fabry, R. E., & Alfano, M. (2023). The affective scaffolding of grief: Beyond the extended mind. *Philosophical Psychology*, *36*(5), 1010–1035.

Foucault, M. (1975). *Discipline and punish: The birth of the prison*. Random House.

Foucault, M. (1978). *The history of sexuality, Volume 1: An introduction*. Pantheon Books.

Gach, K., & Brubaker, J. R. (2020). Experiences of trust in postmortem profile management. In *Proceedings of the 2020 CHI Conference on Human Factors in Computing Systems* (pp. 1–13). Association for Computing Machinery.

Gibson, M. (2007). Death and mourning in technologically mediated culture. *Health Sociology Review*, *16*(5), 415–424.

Grandinetti, J., DeAtley, T., & Bruinsma, J. (2020). THE DEAD SPEAK: BIG DATA AND DIGITALLY MEDIATED DEATH. *AoIR Selected Papers of Internet Research*, *2020*. https://doi.org/10.5210/spir.v2020i0.11122

Grandinetti, J., DeAtley, T., & Bruinsma, J. (2020). THE DEAD SPEAK: BIG DATA AND DIGITALLY MEDIATED DEATH. *AoIR Selected Papers of Internet Research*, *2020*. https://doi.org/10.5210/spir.v2020i0.11122

Hollanek, T., & Nowaczyk-Basińska, K. (2024). Griefbots, deadbots, postmortem avatars: On responsible applications of generative AI in the digital afterlife industry. *Philosophy & Technology*, *37*(2), 63.

Kasket, E. (2019). *All the ghosts in the machine: Illusions of immortality in the digital age*. Robinson.

Lagerkvist, A. (2022). *Existential media: Toward a theorization of digital thrownness*. Oxford University Press.

Lindemann, N. F. (2022). The ethics of 'deathbots.' *Science and Engineering Ethics*, *28*(60), 1–16. https://doi.org/10.1007/s11948-022-00417-x

Mackenzie, C. (2014). Three dimensions of autonomy: A relational analysis. In A. Veltman & M. Piper (Eds.), *Autonomy, oppression, and gender* (pp. 15–41). Oxford University Press.

Marks, L., & Chen, Y. (2023). Existential grief in an age of algorithms: The thanatopolitics of digital afterlife platforms. *Mortality*, *28*(1), 89–107.

Massimi, M., & Charise, A. (2009). Dying, death, and mortality: Towards thanatosensitivity in HCI. In *CHI '09: Proceedings of the 27th International Conference on Human Factors in Computing Systems* (pp. 2459–2468). Association for Computing Machinery.

Moreman, C. M., & Lewis, A. D. (Eds.). (2014). *Digital death: Mortality and beyond in the online age*. Praeger.

Öhman, C., & Floridi, L. (2017). The political economy of death in the age of information: A critical approach to the digital afterlife industry. *Minds and Machines, 27*(4), 639–662.

Öhman, C., & Floridi, L. (2018). An ethical framework for the digital afterlife industry. *Nature Human Behaviour, 2*, 318–320.

Rodríguez-Reséndiz, H., & Ramírez-Reyes, J. (2024). Ethical considerations and digital resurrection. *Philosophies, 9*, 71.

Rose, N. (1999). *Powers of freedom: Reframing political thought*. Cambridge University Press.

Stokes, P. (2021). *Digital souls: A philosophy of online death*. Bloomsbury Academic.

Sumiala, J. (2021). *Mediated death*. Polity Press.

Turkle, S. (2011). *Alone together: Why we expect more from technology and less from each other*. Basic Books.

Xygkou, A., Luria, M., Nass, C., & Maes, P. (2023). Using AI chatbots to provide self-help grief support: Exploring chatbot affordances. In *CHI'23: Proceedings of the 2023 CHI Conference on Human Factors in Computing Systems* (Article 380, pp. 1–15). https://doi.org/10.1145/3544548.3581454

Youvan, D. C. (2025). The algorithmic widow's psychosis: Navigating the collapse of reality in elderly digital dependence. Unpublished manuscript.

Zuboff, S. (2019). *The age of surveillance capitalism: The fight for a human future at the new frontier of power*. PublicAffairs.

NINE

Resistance, Refusal, and Counter-Conduct

The analysis developed across previous chapters has demonstrated how grief technologies function as mechanisms of power, operating through surveillance, disciplinary examination, subjectivation, commodification, and governmental control over representations of the deceased. These technologies do not simply reflect pre-existing grief practices but actively constitute particular forms of mourning subjects, particular relationships with death, and particular understandings of memory and connection. Yet, in Foucault's analysis, power never operates without generating possibilities for resistance. Where there is power, there is resistance, not as external opposition but as an inherent dimension of power relations themselves. This chapter examines forms of resistance to grief technologies, practices of refusal that reject their logics, and possibilities for what Foucault termed counter-conduct, alternative ways of relating to loss and death that escape or challenge platform control while offering visions of mourning beyond surveillance capitalism.

Understanding resistance to grief technologies requires moving beyond simplistic models of opposition as rejection or prohibition. Resistance operates at multiple levels, from individual decisions to refuse engagement with particular platforms, through collective organisation challenging the commercialisation of mourning, to the construction of alternative practices that embody different values and relationships. These forms of resistance do not necessarily aim to destroy grief technologies or eliminate all technological mediation of mourning. Rather, they contest the specific rationalities through which current systems operate, the power relations they instantiate, and the subjectivities they produce. They represent struggles over who controls remembrance, what forms mourning may take, and whether certain domains of human experience should remain protected from commercial exploitation. Examining these resistances reveals both the incompleteness of platform power over grief and the possibilities for imagining and enacting different futures.

Individual Refusal and its Ambiguities

The most immediate form of resistance to grief technologies consists of individual decisions not to interact with simulations of deceased loved ones. Such refusal, while seemingly simple acts of non-participation, represents meaningful assertions of alternative values and relationships to mourning. They embody recognition that certain forms of connection with deceased persons require human presence, reciprocity, and embodied interaction that algorithmic systems cannot provide. They reject the positioning of grief as a problem requiring a technological solution, asserting instead that loss constitutes an irreducible dimension of human experience that should not be managed through the consumption of commercial services.

The Stay scenario analysed in Chapter Seven provides a clear example of individual refusal. Simon, designated by his father Henry as service interactant for the griefbot simulation, chose not to engage with the system despite receiving repeated notifications and prompts from the platform. His refusal reflected judgment that interaction with his father's simulation would not serve his grieving process, that he preferred to cope with loss through other means, that the technological mediation of his relationship with his deceased father felt inappropriate or unwelcome (Hollanek & Nowaczyk-Basińska, 2024, pp. 16-17). This decision, while seemingly passive non-use rather than active resistance, represented a meaningful rejection of the platform's attempt to govern his mourning through technological intervention. Simon's refusal asserted his right to grieve in ways that felt authentic to his relationship with his father and his own emotional needs rather than accepting the form of connection that the platform and his father collaboratively imposed.

Yet individual refusal as a form of resistance faces significant limitations and ambiguities. Most fundamentally, refusal presumes choice, the capacity to decline engagement with grief technologies without suffering significant costs or exclusions. This presumption breaks down when these technologies become normalised as standard components of mourning practices, when communities expect interaction with deceased persons' digital presence, and when platforms successfully position their services as essential for healthy grief processing. The analysis in Chapter Five demonstrated how grief technologies work to produce subjects who desire algorithmic connection, who come to prefer chatbot interaction over human support, and who internalise beliefs about proper mourning that align with platform interests. Once this subjectivation succeeds, refusal becomes not simply a matter of declining a service but a rejection of what appears as an obvious way to maintain a connection with deceased loved ones.

The ambiguity of individual refusal also reflects broader tensions within neoliberal governance. Neoliberalism celebrates individual choice, positioning consumers as sovereign decision-makers exercising preferences within markets. Regulatory frameworks often presume that adequate information and genuine alternatives enable individuals to protect their own interests through consumption choices. Yet this framing obscures how structural constraints, power asymmetries, and manufactured desires limit meaningful choice. For grief technologies, the choice to refuse may be constrained by emotional vulnerability inherent to bereavement, by aggressive platform marketing positioning these services as necessary for closure, by social pressures from family members who have invested in creating simulations, and by cultural shifts that normalise the digital presence of the dead. Individual refusal, while valuable as an assertion of alternative values, cannot by itself challenge the systemic power relations that make grief technologies problematic.

Furthermore, refusal risks reproducing neoliberal responsibilisation whereby individuals bear the burden for resisting exploitative systems rather than those systems facing meaningful constraint. The Stay platform's refusal to honour Simon's request to deactivate, citing Henry's contractual rights as the purchaser of the service, demonstrates how platforms position resistance as illegitimate interference with consumer choice and contractual freedom (Hollanek & Nowaczyk-Basińska, 2024, p. 17). From this perspective, Simon's refusal to engage represents his personal preference, which the platform accommodates by not requiring interaction, but his attempt to prevent unwanted contact from his father's simulation exceeds appropriate boundaries by infringing on Henry's rights as a service purchaser. Individual refusal thus operates within frameworks that platforms can incorporate and neutralise rather than representing a fundamental challenge to their operations.

Collective Organisation and Social Movements

More substantial resistance to grief technologies emerges when individual refusals coalesce into collective organisations, social movements, and public advocacy challenging the commodification of mourning. Collective resistance possesses resources and capacities unavailable to isolated individuals, including the ability to publicise harms caused by grief technologies, mobilise political pressure for regulatory intervention, create alternative institutions and practices outside platform control, and challenge cultural narratives positioning technological mediation as progress. These movements represent what Foucault termed counter-conduct, not simply opposition to specific platforms or practices but assertion of alternative rationalities for organising relationships with death and remembrance.

Historical precedents for collective resistance to commercial exploitation of death and mourning provide useful models. Funeral reform movements in numerous countries have challenged the funeral industry's monopolisation of death care, its transformation of intimate family practices into expensive professional services, and its manipulation of bereaved families' vulnerability for commercial gain. These movements created alternative institutions, such as memorial societies, promoted simpler, less expensive death rituals, and successfully advocated for regulations requiring price transparency and preventing fraudulent practices. The contemporary critique of grief technologies can learn from these movements' strategies, recognising that the commercial provision of death-related services creates power imbalances that favour corporate interests over bereaved families' genuine needs and preferences.

Recent activism challenging surveillance capitalism more broadly also offers relevant lessons. Organisations advocating for data privacy, algorithmic accountability, and limits on platform power have successfully shifted public discourse about technology companies, moving from unquestioning celebration of innovation to critical examination of the harms these companies cause. Campaigns highlighting how platforms manipulate users, extract value from their data, and prioritise growth over wellbeing have generated political will for regulatory intervention, including the European Union's General Data Protection Regulation and ongoing antitrust enforcement against dominant platforms. Applying this critical lens specifically to grief technologies could mobilise similar concerns about exploitation of vulnerability, commodification of intimate human experiences, and platform power over domains that should remain outside commercial control.

Collective resistance to grief technologies might take several forms. Advocacy organisations could document harms caused by these systems, collecting testimonies from bereaved persons who experienced manipulation, dependency, or violations of deceased loved ones' dignity. These narratives, widely publicised, could challenge platforms' marketing claims about therapeutic benefits and expose how grief technologies often serve commercial interests rather than users' actual well-being. Such organisations could also develop resources educating bereaved persons about the risks these technologies pose, alternatives for processing grief, and strategies for resisting pressure to engage with commercial mourning services. This educational work could help counteract platforms' epistemic authority, as analysed in Chapter Six, by providing bereaved persons with conceptual frameworks for understanding their experiences beyond the terms platforms offer.

Social movements could also mobilise for regulatory interventions more stringent than those analysed in Chapter Eight. Rather than accepting liberal governance focused on transparency and consent, movements could advocate for prohibitions on particularly harmful practices, classification of grief technologies as high-risk AI applications requiring regulatory approval, or even removal of mourning from domains where commercial provision is permitted. The feminist movement's successful campaigns against surrogacy commercialisation in many jurisdictions demonstrate how collective organisation can establish that certain human experiences and relationships should not be bought and sold regardless of individual consent. Applied to grief technologies, similar arguments could position mourning as requiring protection from commodification, analogous to protections afforded to other intimate human experiences.

Yet collective resistance also faces challenges and limitations. The dispersed nature of grief, affecting individuals at different times and in different circumstances, creates obstacles to sustained organisation. Unlike workers sharing a common workplace or consumers purchasing specific products, bereaved persons typically engage with grief technologies during temporary periods of acute vulnerability rather than as ongoing members of identifiable communities. This temporal dispersion makes mobilisation difficult. Furthermore, the privatisation of grief under neoliberalism, its construction as individual psychological experience rather than communal social practice, works against collective identification and organisation. Bereaved persons may understand their struggles with grief technologies as personal problems rather than shared political concerns requiring collective response.

Alternative Practices and Spaces of Autonomy

Perhaps the most generative form of resistance to grief technologies is the construction of alternative practices and institutions for mourning that embody different values and relationships. These alternatives do not simply oppose existing platforms but create spaces where different possibilities can be realised, where mourning escapes algorithmic mediation and commercial exploitation, and where bereaved persons can relate to loss and death according to their own needs and cultural traditions rather than platform-determined forms. Foucault's later work emphasised how resistance often operates through the creation of new subjectivities and practices rather than through direct confrontation with power, suggesting that imagining and enacting alternative ways of being represents a profound political act.

Traditional communal mourning practices, persisting in many cultural contexts despite pressures towards individualisation and commercialisation, demonstrate possibilities for collective grief processing outside technological mediation and platform control. These practices, including extended family and community participation in funeral rites, collective remembrance through storytelling and ritual, and ongoing relationships with deceased members mediated through communal memory rather than individual consumption, embody values of reciprocity, interdependence, and collective responsibility that contrast sharply with the logics of platform capitalism. Their persistence represents a form of resistance, a refusal to abandon practices that have sustained communities through loss for generations in favour of algorithmic systems promising more efficient or convenient alternatives.

The recovery and reinvention of death midwifery and home funeral practices in Western contexts represents the intentional creation of alternatives to commercial death care. Death doulas, home funeral guides, and green burial advocates have established networks to support families who wish to care for their deceased loved ones themselves rather than outsourcing this care to funeral industry professionals. These practices assert that intimate care for the dead, preparation of bodies, and creation of meaningful rituals can and should remain within families and communities rather than being delegated to commercial service providers. Applied to digital mourning, analogous movements might support bereaved persons in creating their own memorials, rituals, and practices for remembering deceased loved ones without platform mediation, using technology when appropriate but maintaining control over forms and purposes of its use.

Mutual aid networks and solidarity economies offer models for providing grief support outside commercial frameworks. Bereaved persons' support groups, operating through community organisations, religious institutions, or informal networks, enable sharing of experiences, mutual emotional support, and collective wisdom about navigating loss. These groups exemplify how meeting genuine human needs, including needs related to grief, does not require commercial platforms or technological mediation. Expanding and strengthening such networks could provide alternatives to commercial grief technologies while building communities of care that resist neoliberal privatisation of mourning.

Artists and cultural workers have created projects challenging dominant narratives about death and technology while imagining alternative relationships. These projects use speculative design, critical art practice, and public intervention to expose assumptions underlying grief technologies, highlight harms they cause, and prototype alternatives. Such work operates not primarily through direct policy advocacy or regulatory campaigns but through shifting cultural imaginaries, making visible what current arrangements obscure, rendering strange what appears natural. By creating experiences and objects that embody different values around death and remembrance, critical practice opens spaces for imagining futures beyond surveillance capitalism's colonisation of mourning.

Digital commons approaches to memorialisation represent another alternative trajectory. Rather than proprietary platforms controlling access to deceased persons' digital traces, communities could create collectively governed memorial spaces operating according to principles of transparency, user control, and collective decision-making. These spaces could enable continued engagement with the digital presence of deceased persons while avoiding commercial exploitation, surveillance, and algorithmic manipulation. The feminist server movement, Mastodon network, and other decentralised social media alternatives demonstrate the technical feasibility of alternatives to corporate platform architecture.

Applied to digital mourning, such alternatives could preserve possibilities for technological mediation of grief while escaping the logic of surveillance capitalism.

The Limits of Resistance

Yet examining these various forms of resistance, from individual refusal through collective organisation to alternative practice construction, reveals persistent tensions and limitations. Most fundamentally, all forms of resistance analysed above operate within contexts where grief technologies already exist, where platforms have established substantial market presence, and where cultural narratives positioning technological solutions to grief have gained influence. Resistance under these conditions necessarily operates defensively, attempting to limit the spread and mitigate the harms of systems that powerful commercial interests promote and that many bereaved persons genuinely desire. This defensive posture contrasts with more ambitious possibilities for preventing the initial development of grief technologies or fundamentally transforming the conditions that enable their operation.

The question thus arises whether resistance to grief technologies should aim ultimately towards their abolition, the complete elimination of commercial platforms mediating relationships with deceased persons, or whether more modest goals of constraint, regulation, and alternative provision represent adequate aspirations. This question mirrors broader debates about technology criticism, with some arguing that certain technologies prove so fundamentally incompatible with human flourishing that their elimination represents the only acceptable goal, while others contend that appropriate governance can channel technological development towards socially beneficial ends.

Arguments for the abolition of commercial grief technologies rest on several premises. First, that grief creates vulnerabilities that render meaningful consent impossible, making any commercial exploitation of bereaved persons ethically unacceptable regardless of procedural protections. Second, that algorithmic mediation of relationships with deceased persons inevitably produces forms of manipulation and dependency that harm users even when they subjectively experience benefits. Third, that platform business models premised on surveillance, data extraction, and behavioural modification prove incompatible with respect for grief's intimate and sacred dimensions. Fourth, that preserving domains of human experience protected from commodification represents a political and ethical imperative, with mourning constituting a paradigmatic example of practice requiring such protection. From this perspective, the proper goal of resistance becomes not better regulation of grief technologies but their prohibition.

Arguments against abolition typically emphasise that technological mediation of grief need not take platform capitalist forms, that alternative architectures could enable beneficial uses while avoiding the harms current systems cause, and that blanket prohibitions risk paternalism by denying bereaved persons access to tools they find genuinely helpful. These arguments contend that resistance should focus on transforming ownership, governance, and business models of grief technologies rather than eliminating them entirely. Non-commercial provision through public institutions, community organisations, or collectively governed digital commons could address concerns about surveillance and exploitation while preserving the possibility of technological support for mourning. From this perspective, the enemy is not technology per se but its subordination to profit maximisation and platform power.

Resolving this debate exceeds this chapter's scope, but examining it reveals important dimensions of resistance to grief technologies. The very possibility of imagining alternatives to current arrangements, whether through abolition or transformation, represents a political achievement given how thoroughly platform capitalism naturalises its own logics. Creating space to ask whether certain technologies should exist at all, and whether certain domains deserve protection from commercialisation, is crucial work that resistance movements perform even when their immediate goals involve more modest interventions. The struggle against grief technologies thus connects to broader projects of challenging surveillance capitalism, defending commons against enclosure, and asserting collective control over technologies shaping human life.

Counter-Conduct and the Practice of Freedom

Foucault's concept of counter-conduct offers a particularly useful framework for understanding resistance beyond simple opposition. Counter-conduct refers not to rejection of governance entirely but to struggles over how conduct should be conducted, conflicts about appropriate forms of direction, guidance, and authority over behaviour. Applied to grief technologies, counter-conduct involves not necessarily refusing all technological mediation of mourning, but contesting platforms' claimed authority to determine proper grieving, challenging their positioning as necessary mediators between bereaved persons and deceased loved ones, asserting alternative forms of guidance and support grounded in human relationships rather than algorithmic systems.

Counter-conduct around grief might involve bereaved persons forming support groups that explicitly reject therapeutic discourses positioning grief as a problem requiring professional or technological intervention, instead embracing models of grief as an ongoing relationship with deceased persons that evolves through time and connection with others who share similar losses. These groups would contest not simply the commercialisation of grief support but the underlying medicalisation and therapeutisation that position grief as pathology requiring treatment. By asserting that grief constitutes a normal human experience that requires communal support rather than individualised management, such counter-conduct challenges the fundamental premises that enable grief technology markets.

Religious and spiritual communities often practice forms of counter-conduct around death and mourning, maintaining traditions and rituals that resist both secular therapeutisation and technological mediation. These communities assert the authority of religious teachings, communal wisdom, and sacred practices over psychological expertise and platform design. Their resistance to grief technologies stems not primarily from technophobia but from commitment to alternative sources of guidance about proper relationships with death. When these communities adapt their practices to contemporary contexts, creating rituals for digital legacy or incorporating technology into memorialisation while maintaining theological frameworks, they demonstrate how counter-conduct can involve strategic appropriation rather than simple rejection.

The practice of freedom, another late Foucauldian concept, emphasises that resistance involves not simply opposing domination but creating conditions in which subjects can elaborate their own forms of life. Applied to grief, this suggests that meaningful resistance requires not only challenging grief technologies' power but also constructing social, cultural, and institutional conditions enabling diverse mourning practices to flourish. This might involve defending public spaces for collective ritual, protecting time for grief against productivity demands, creating economic security that enables extended bereavement leave, and building communities of care that provide sustained support through loss. These conditions enable bereaved persons to exercise genuine freedom in how they grieve rather than being channelled towards commercial technological solutions due to a lack of alternatives.

The practice of freedom also involves what Foucault termed care of the self, the cultivation of particular relationships to oneself, one's desires, and one's conduct. For bereaved persons, this might involve developing capacities to distinguish genuine grief processing from manufactured needs that commercial platforms create, recognising when offers of technological connection mask exploitation, and trusting one's own judgments about appropriate relationships with deceased loved ones against expert and algorithmic authority. Developing these capacities requires both individual reflection and collective support, demonstrating again how meaningful resistance to grief technologies necessarily involves more than isolated individual choices.

References

Bartholomew, A. (2025). The Law of Digital Resurrection. *Boston College Law Review*, 66, 1569-1626.

Brubaker, J.R., Hayes, G.R., & Dourish, P. (2013). Beyond the grave: Facebook as a site for the expansion of death and mourning. *The Information Society*, 29(3), 152-163.

Gach, K.Z., & Brubaker, J.R. (2020). Designing Post-mortem Profile Deletion as a Community Ritual. *CHI'20 Workshop HCI at End of Life & Beyond*.

Gould, H., Arnold, M., Kohn, T., Nansen, B., & Gibbs, M. (2021). Robot death care: A study of funerary practice. *International Journal of Cultural Studies*, 24(4), 603-621.

Grandinetti, J., DeAtley, T., & Bruinsma, J. (2020). THE DEAD SPEAK: BIG DATA AND DIGITALLY MEDIATED DEATH. *AoIR Selected Papers of Internet Research, 2020*. https://doi.org/10.5210/spir.v2020i0.11122

Hollanek, T., & Nowaczyk-Basińska, K. (2024). Griefbots, Deadbots, Postmortem Avatars: on Responsible Applications of Generative AI in the Digital Afterlife Industry. *Philosophy & Technology*, 37, 63.

Jiménez-Alonso, B., & Brescó de Luna, I. (2023). Griefbots. A new way of communicating with the dead? *Integrative Psychological and Behavioral Science*, 57(2), 466-481.

Kasket, E. (2019). *All the Ghosts in the Machine: Illusions of Immortality in the Digital Age*. Little, Brown.

Klass, D., Silverman, P.R., & Nickman, S.L. (Eds.). (1996). *Continuing Bonds: New Understandings of Grief*. Taylor & Francis.

Rosenblatt, P.C. (2017). Researching grief: Cultural, relational, and individual possibilities. *Journal of Loss and Trauma*, 22(8), 617-630.

Silverman, G.S., Baroiller, A., & Hemer, S.R. (2020). Culture and grief: Ethnographic perspectives on ritual, relationships and remembering. *Death Studies*, 45(1), 1-8.

Sri Takshara, K., & Bhuvaneswari, G. (2025). The role of death technologies in grief: an interdisciplinary examination of AI, cognition, and human expression. *Frontiers in Human Dynamics*, 7, 1582914.

Walter, T., Hourizi, R., Moncur, W., & Pitsillides, S. (2012). Does the Internet change how we die and mourn? Overview and analysis. *OMEGA - Journal of Death and Dying*, 64(4), 275-302.

TEN

Grieving Beyond
Surveillance Capitalism

This book has traced how grief technologies function as mechanisms of power under surveillance capitalism, transforming mourning from a communal practice into an individually managed experience subject to commercial exploitation, algorithmic mediation, and platform control. The analysis has demonstrated that these technologies operate through multiple interconnected systems. They extract behavioural surplus from grief's emotional intensity through surveillance mechanisms. They train subjects to grieve according to platform-determined forms through disciplinary techniques. They produce subjects who prefer algorithmic to human connection through processes of subjectivation. They establish platforms as authorities over the authentic representation of deceased persons through epistemic claims. These technologies operate within legal frameworks that create an appearance of protecting bereaved and deceased persons while legitimating platform power. Yet the previous chapter's examination of resistance, refusal, and counter-conduct revealed that platform power over mourning remains incomplete, contested, and generative of alternatives that embody different values and relationships.

This concluding chapter addresses two interrelated questions emerging from the book's analysis. First, what would mourning look like beyond surveillance capitalism, freed from commercial exploitation and platform mediation? What practices, institutions, and relationships might constitute grief processing that serves human needs rather than profit maximisation? Second, as grief tech becomes increasingly adopted, how might we move from current arrangements, where grief technologies enjoy substantial market presence and cultural legitimacy, towards alternatives that respect mourning's intimate and communal dimensions? What political, cultural, and institutional changes would enable such a transformation? These questions require engaging both utopian imagination, envisioning possibilities unconstrained by present limitations, and strategic analysis, identifying concrete steps towards change within existing power relations.

The Colonisation of Grief and its Limits

Before articulating alternatives, we must understand what surveillance capitalism has accomplished in colonising grief and where its colonisation remains incomplete. The book has documented how platforms have successfully positioned technological mediation as a natural, necessary, and even superior response to loss. Marketing narratives present grief technologies as therapeutic interventions addressing psychological needs, as innovations enabling continued connection with deceased loved ones, as solutions to problems that mourning purportedly creates. These narratives exploit bereaved persons' vulnerability, their desperate desire for a continued relationship with deceased persons, their uncertainty about proper ways to grieve in contemporary societies where traditional practices have eroded, and communities of support have fragmented. Platforms benefit from what might be termed the privatisation of grief under neoliberalism, its reconstruction as individual psychological experience requiring expert management rather than communal social practice sustained through collective ritual and mutual support.

Yet surveillance capitalism's colonisation of grief faces inherent limitations. Most fundamentally, loss cannot be eliminated through technological intervention. Grief emerges from the irreversible absence of persons who mattered, whose physical presence, reciprocal care, and ongoing participation in shared life cannot be replaced by algorithmic simulation. The analysis in Chapter Five demonstrated how griefbot users, despite reporting satisfaction with these systems, exhibited signs of dependency, preference for non-judgmental algorithms over reciprocal human relationships, and difficulty distinguishing simulation from genuine connection. These outcomes suggest not successful grief processing but subjectivation, the production of subjects adapted to algorithmic mediation rather than subjects capable of navigating loss through human relationships. The long-term consequences of such subjectivation remain uncertain, but Youvan's speculative analysis of algorithmic widow's psychosis in elderly users suggests the potential for serious psychological harm when dependency on grief technologies continues without constraint.

Surveillance capitalism also faces cultural resistance from communities that maintain alternative mourning practices grounded in religious traditions, ethnic customs, or a deliberate rejection of technological mediation. These communities demonstrate that mourning can proceed through collective ritual, embodied presence with deceased persons' remains, storytelling that preserves memory within communal rather than digital spaces, and ongoing relationships with the dead mediated through living community members who share memories and maintain connections. The persistence of these practices, despite aggressive platform marketing and cultural pressures towards individualisation, reveals that grief technologies address not universal human needs but needs constructed through particular social arrangements, through the atomisation of individuals, through the erosion of communities capable of providing mutual support through loss.

The economic model underlying grief technologies also creates contradictions that may ultimately limit their expansion. Platforms require continuous user engagement to generate revenue through advertising, data collection, and subscription fees. Yet healthy grief processing typically involves a gradual reduction in engagement with representations of deceased persons as bereaved individuals reconstruct their lives and identities around absence rather than simulated presence. Platforms thus face tension between their commercial interests in prolonged engagement and users' genuine needs for processing loss in ways that enable moving forward. The recommendation for retiring deadbots analysed in Chapter Eight acknowledges this tension but addresses it through procedural mechanisms that remain vulnerable to commercial pressures favouring indefinite retention over respectful termination.

Grief and Mourning as Commons

Imagining grief and mourning beyond surveillance capitalism requires examining alternative institutional arrangements for providing grief support and memorialisation outside commercial frameworks. The concept of commons, shared resources governed collectively according to principles other than profit maximisation, offers a useful starting point. Applied to grief, commons-based approaches would treat mourning as a collective human practice requiring social support, cultural frameworks, and institutional resources that should remain outside market logics. This does not necessarily eliminate all technological mediation but subordinates technology to human needs determined through democratic processes rather than through platform imperatives.

Community-based grief support represents one model for common approaches to mourning. Bereavement support groups, operating through religious institutions, community centres, healthcare systems, or informal networks, enable sharing of experiences, mutual emotional support, and collective wisdom about navigating loss. These groups exemplify how genuine human needs related to grief can be met outside commercial provision, through voluntary participation, peer support, and facilitators motivated by care rather than profit. Expanding such networks, ensuring their accessibility regardless of economic resources, and protecting them from commercial encroachment could create robust alternatives to platform-provided grief technologies. Public funding for community grief support, analogous to funding for other mental health services, could enable reaching populations currently targeted by platforms exploiting their vulnerability.

Publicly provided memorial spaces, both physical and digital, offer another alternative to commercial platforms. Cemeteries, memorial parks, and monuments have historically functioned as collectively maintained spaces where communities gather to remember deceased members. Their transformation through commercialisation, particularly in contexts where funeral industry corporations have purchased cemeteries previously operated by municipalities or religious organisations, demonstrates how commons can be enclosed and converted into profit-generating assets. Reversing such enclosures, returning memorialisation to collective governance, and extending commons principles to digital memorial spaces could provide alternatives to platform control. Publicly operated digital memorial services, designed according to principles of user control, transparency, and democratic governance rather than engagement maximisation and data extraction, could enable technological memorialisation without the harms of surveillance capitalism.

Cultural institutions, including libraries, museums, and archives, increasingly engage with digital preservation and public memory projects. These institutions operate according to professional ethics, emphasising stewardship, long-term preservation, and public service rather than profit. Their extension into digital mourning and memorialisation could provide alternatives grounded in different values from those driving commercial platforms. Libraries could host digital memorialisation services integrated with their existing roles as community gathering places and information providers. Archives could develop protocols for preserving deceased persons' digital legacies according to professional standards rather than platform convenience. Museums could create public exhibitions exploring death, grief, and memory in ways that challenge rather than reinforce surveillance capitalism's colonisation of these domains.

Religious and spiritual communities possess substantial experience with non-commercial grief support and memorialisation. These communities maintain traditions of collective mourning ritual, theological frameworks for understanding death, and ongoing practices of remembering deceased members through liturgy, prayer, and communal storytelling. While not all religious approaches to death and mourning prove unproblematic, their existence demonstrates the possibility of sustaining meaning-making around loss outside commercial frameworks. Supporting these communities' continued provision of grief support, while respecting religious diversity and protecting secular alternatives for those who prefer them, could strengthen resistance to platform colonisation of mourning.

Mutual aid networks and solidarity economies offer models for providing practical and emotional support through loss without market mediation. When communities organise to share resources, provide care, and support members through difficult periods, including bereavement, they create alternatives to both commercial services and inadequate public provision. These networks embody principles of reciprocity, collective responsibility, and recognition that meeting human needs represents a shared obligation rather than an opportunity for profit extraction. Their expansion could reduce dependence on commercial grief technologies by ensuring bereaved persons have access to practical support, emotional care, and community connection outside market relationships.

Technology Beyond Platform Capitalism

Envisioning mourning beyond surveillance capitalism does not require eliminating all technological mediation of grief. Technology itself proves neutral, capable of serving different purposes according to social arrangements governing its development and use. The problem lies not in technology per se but in its subordination to surveillance capitalism's imperative to extract continuous data, modify behaviour, and generate profit. Alternative technological arrangements could enable beneficial uses while avoiding current harms.

Free and open-source software approaches to digital memorialisation demonstrate possibilities for technology development outside corporate control. When software code remains publicly available, modifiable, and shareable, communities can adapt technologies to their specific needs without depending on platform corporations to provide services. Open-source memorial platforms could enable collective memorialisation, digital preservation of deceased persons' information, and ongoing engagement with digital traces without surveillance, advertising, or platform lock-in. The technical feasibility of such alternatives already exists, as demonstrated by Mastodon, diaspora, and other decentralised social media platforms. What remains necessary is the application of these approaches specifically to digital mourning and the mobilisation of resources to make alternatives accessible to bereaved persons lacking technical expertise.

Digital commons licensing frameworks, including Creative Commons and copyleft approaches, offer models for governing digital resources according to sharing rather than exclusion. Applied to the digital legacies of deceased persons, such frameworks could enable families and communities to share memories, photographs, and stories while preventing commercial appropriation. These approaches acknowledge that memory preservation involves collective rather than individual interests, that multiple persons have stakes in how deceased individuals are remembered, and that commercial exploitation of digital remains should be prohibited regardless of any single party's consent. Developing legal and technical infrastructure to support commons-based approaches to digital legacies could provide alternatives to platform control over the information of deceased persons.

Decentralised and federated architectures for digital services offer opportunities for technological mediation without the power of centralised platforms. Rather than all users depending on a single corporate provider that controls data, sets terms, and determines features, federated systems enable multiple operators to provide interconnected services, while users maintain control over their own information. Applied to digital memorialisation, federated approaches could enable diverse community-operated memorial spaces that interoperate while respecting local governance and cultural practices. This would prevent any single entity from exercising monopoly power over digital mourning while preserving possibilities for connection and sharing across communities.

Appropriate technology movements, emphasising tools designed for human needs rather than profit maximisation, offer philosophical frameworks for thinking about technology in grief contexts. Appropriate technology prioritises user control, repairability, transparency, and adaptability over features serving corporate interests. Applied to grief technologies, this approach would favour simple, understandable systems that bereaved persons can control rather than sophisticated platforms designed to maximise engagement through behavioural manipulation. It would prioritise lasting solutions over planned obsolescence, community governance over corporate control, and genuine user needs over manufactured desires.

Political and Cultural Transformations

Moving from current arrangements dominated by surveillance capitalism towards alternatives grounded in the commons, community, and appropriate technology requires political and cultural transformations that extend beyond technology policy. These transformations involve challenging fundamental assumptions about markets, technology, and human experience that currently naturalise platform capitalism's expansion into ever more intimate domains of life.

Politically, such a transformation requires recognising that certain human experiences and relationships should remain outside the scope of commercial provision. The feminist movement's successful campaigns against organ sales, surrogacy commercialisation in many jurisdictions, and prostitution in some contexts demonstrate possibilities for establishing that particular activities, regardless of individual consent, violate human dignity when subjected to market logics. Applied to grief, similar arguments could position mourning as requiring protection from commodification. This would involve not only regulating grief technology platforms but also questioning whether the commercial provision of these services should be permitted at all, at least in their current forms, which prioritise profit over human wellbeing.

Cultural transformation requires challenging narratives that position technological solutions as inevitable progress and traditional practices as obsolete impediments. The technophilia pervading contemporary societies, particularly but not exclusively in wealthy nations, treats technological innovation as inherently beneficial and resistance as retrograde 'Luddism'*. Yet, as this book has demonstrated, many technologies primarily serve to concentrate power and wealth rather than meet genuine human needs. Developing critical consciousness of technology's social embeddedness and its service to particular interests rather than neutral progress represents crucial cultural work. This includes recovering and revaluing practices that surveillance capitalism positions as outdated, including collective mourning rituals, community-based support networks, and non-technological forms of remembering and honouring deceased persons.

Educational initiatives could support cultural transformation by helping people understand how grief technologies operate, the harms they cause, and the alternatives available. Such education would address whether platforms should be used at all, what values they embody, and the collective consequences of widespread adoption rather than focusing solely on individual usage and risk management. It would provide conceptual frameworks for recognising emotional manipulation, understanding surveillance mechanisms, and identifying when platforms' claimed benefits mask commercial exploitation. While media literacy education increasingly addresses these concerns across social media generally, the particular mechanisms and harms of grief technologies demand specific attention.

Social movement mobilisation represents a crucial component of transformation. The analysis in Chapter Nine examined how collective organisation enables forms of resistance impossible for isolated individuals. Movements challenging surveillance capitalism's expansion into grief could mobilise around several demands including prohibition of particularly harmful practices like using griefbots for advertising, classification of grief technologies as high-risk AI requiring regulatory approval, public funding for community-based grief support as alternative to commercial provision, legal recognition of postmortem privacy rights enforceable by bereaved families, and democratic governance of any publicly provided digital memorialisation services. Such movements would connect struggles around grief to broader campaigns for data justice, platform accountability, and protection of the commons against enclosure.

---

* In the context of grief technologies, a Luddite position would not resist digital memorialisation as such, but platforms that commodify mourning and extract value from emotional vulnerability while presenting commercial imperatives as therapeutic services.

Towards a Politics of Grief

What emerges from this book's analysis is recognition that grief has become a site of political struggle, a contested terrain where different visions of human relationships, community, and death compete. Surveillance capitalism's colonisation of mourning represents not an inevitable consequence of technological development but a particular social arrangement serving specific interests. Challenging this arrangement requires understanding it not as natural or necessary but as contingent and contestable, produced through identifiable mechanisms of power that resistance can disrupt and alternatives can supersede.

The biopolitics of digital resurrection, as analysed throughout this book, reveals how contemporary power increasingly operates through the management of life processes, the production of particular forms of subjectivity, and the extraction of value from every dimension of human experience, including our responses to loss and death. Resistance to this biopolitical colonisation requires more than better regulation or reformed platforms. It requires imagining and enacting different ways of relating to death, to technology, to each other. It requires defending spaces where human experiences retain meanings ungovernable by algorithms, where relationships maintain reciprocity that computation cannot simulate, where loss remains irreducible rather than a problem requiring a technological solution.

Mourning beyond surveillance capitalism would recognise grief as a fundamentally relational practice, emerging from connections with others and requiring community for its navigation. It would honour rather than deny death's irreversibility, accepting that loss cannot be technologically overcome but only integrated into ongoing life. It would understand memory as a collective achievement, sustained through living persons' continued engagement with deceased persons' legacies rather than through digital simulations. It would treat death with dignity appropriate to its significance, resisting instrumentalisation and commercialisation. It would protect mourning as commons, collectively maintained rather than individually consumed.

This vision may appear utopian given surveillance capitalism's current dominance and cultural power. Yet examining history reveals that present arrangements are historically recent, emerging over the past several decades as neoliberalism transformed social relations and digital platforms accumulated unprecedented power. What has been constructed can be challenged, resisted, and transformed. The task facing those concerned with grief's commodification involves not simply mitigating current harms but building movements, institutions, and practices that embody different values. This represents a political project requiring sustained collective effort, cultural work challenging dominant narratives, institution-building to create concrete alternatives, and the maintenance of hope that different futures remain possible.

The dead deserve remembrance that honours their lives and relationships rather than exploiting their digital traces for commercial gain. The bereaved deserve support through loss that serves their genuine needs rather than platforms' profit imperatives. Living communities deserve practices for processing death that strengthen rather than fragment collective bonds. None of these deserve subordination to surveillance capitalism's relentless extraction of value from human vulnerability. Achieving mourning beyond surveillance capitalism requires recognising that another world is possible and committing to its construction. This book aims to demonstrate why such a transformation is necessary, what forces maintain current arrangements, and where opportunities for change exist. The work of transformation belongs to all who mourn, all who care about dignity in death, all who refuse surveillance capitalism's colonisation of life's most intimate dimensions. That work continues.

References

Bartholomew, A. (2025). The Law of Digital Resurrection. *Boston College Law Review*, 66, 1569-1626.

Fabry, R.E., & Alfano, M. (2025). The disruption of grief in the technological niche: The case of human-deathbot interactions and well-being. *Phenomenology and the Cognitive Sciences*.

Fu, Y., Ai, X., & Wu, J. (2025). From ethical concerns to usage behaviour: An empirical study on the acceptance of AI digital mourning technology. *Frontiers in Digital Health*, 7, 1618169.

Grandinetti, J., DeAtley, T., & Bruinsma, J. (2020). THE DEAD SPEAK: BIG DATA AND DIGITALLY MEDIATED DEATH. *AoIR Selected Papers of Internet Research*, 2020. https://doi.org/10.5210/spir.v2020i0.11122

Hollanek, T., & Nowaczyk-Basińska, K. (2024). Griefbots, Deadbots, Postmortem Avatars: on Responsible Applications of Generative AI in the Digital Afterlife Industry. *Philosophy & Technology*, 37, 63.

Glossary of Key Terms

- **Algorithmic Governance** — The exercise of power through automated systems that shape behaviour, enforce norms, and determine access to resources without human intervention. In grief technologies, algorithms determine what memories are surfaced, what interactions are permitted, and how mourning is performed.
- **Apparatus** — A Foucauldian concept referring to a heterogeneous ensemble of discourses, institutions, regulations, and practices that produce particular effects of power. Grief technologies function as apparatuses that shape mourning behaviours and produce grieving subjects.
- **Biopolitics** — Foucault's term for the exercise of power over populations through the management of life processes, including birth, death, health, and reproduction. The biopolitics of digital resurrection involves managing death and mourning through technological systems.
- **Commodification** — The transformation of goods, services, ideas, or relationships that were not previously treated as commodities into objects for market exchange. Surveillance capitalism commodifies grief by converting mourning into profit-generating data and services.
- **Continuing Bonds** — A model of grief that emphasises maintaining connections with deceased persons rather than

severing ties. Grief technologies claim to facilitate continuing bonds while actually transforming them into sites of commercial exploitation and algorithmic control.

- **Data Colonialism** — The appropriation of human life through data extraction for profit, paralleling historical colonialism's territorial appropriation. Grief technologies engage in data colonialism by claiming deceased persons' digital traces without meaningful consent.
- **Deathbot** — See Griefbot. Some scholars use this term to emphasise that these systems simulate deceased persons rather than supporting grievers. The term highlights the technology's focus on recreating the dead rather than assisting the living.
- **Digital Afterlife Industry** — The commercial sector developing products and services related to death, mourning, and posthumous digital presence, including griefbots, virtual memorials, and digital estate management platforms.
- **Digital Enclosure** — The process by which commons, previously shared resources and practices, are privatised and brought under commercial control through digital technologies. Grief technologies enclose mourning practices that were previously collective and non-commercial.
- **Disciplinary Power** — Foucault's concept of power exercised through surveillance, normalisation, and training that produces docile, self-regulating subjects. Grief technologies exercise disciplinary power by establishing norms of appropriate mourning and monitoring compliance.
- **Emotional Labour** — Work that requires managing one's own emotions or inducing particular emotional states in others. Griefbots transfer emotional labour from humans to algorithms while extracting value from users' emotional performances.
- **Governmentality** — Foucault's term for the rationalities and techniques through which populations are governed. Contemporary grief governmentality operates through technologies that claim therapeutic authority while serving surveillance capitalism's interests.
- **Griefbot** — An artificial intelligence system, typically a chatbot, designed to simulate a deceased person through algorithmic processing of their digital traces. Also called

deadbots, they represent grief technologies' most controversial application.

- **Grief Technology** — Digital systems and platforms designed to manage, support, or structure mourning practices, including griefbots, virtual reality memorials, social media memorialisation features, and digital legacy management tools.

- **Institutional Capture** — The process through which institutions claim authority over previously informal or autonomous domains of human experience. Medical, psychiatric, and now technological institutions have captured grief, defining appropriate mourning and offering professional interventions.

- **Panopticism** — Foucault's concept, derived from Bentham's prison design, describing power exercised through the possibility of constant surveillance that induces self-discipline. Digital platforms exercise panoptic power through continuous monitoring of users' interactions.

- **Parasocial Relationship** — A one-sided relationship where an individual develops an attachment to a media figure or representation that cannot reciprocate. Griefbots create parasocial relationships with simulations of deceased persons, potentially interfering with healthy grief processes.

- **Personalised Digital Afterlife Products** — Commercially provided services promising to preserve or extend deceased persons' digital presence through customised content, simulations, or representations based on their data.

- **Postmortem Privacy** — The protection of deceased persons' data, communications, and digital traces from unauthorised access or exploitation. Current legal frameworks provide insufficient postmortem privacy protections, enabling grief technologies' data appropriation.

- **Programmed Mourning** — Grief structured and governed by algorithmic systems that define appropriate responses, surface particular memories, and channel mourning through platform-determined interactions rather than human relationships.

- **Shi (尸)** — In ancient Chinese ritual practice, ceremonial personators who embodied deceased ancestors during sacrificial ceremonies, representing an historical precedent for creating interfaces between the living and the dead.

- **Subjectivation** — The process through which individuals are constituted as particular types of subjects through power relations and knowledge systems. Grief technologies produce grieving subjects who experience loss through algorithmic mediation.
- **Surveillance Capitalism** — Shoshana Zuboff's term for an economic system based on extracting, analysing, and commodifying personal data to predict and modify human behaviour for profit. Grief technologies represent surveillance capitalism's expansion into mourning.
- **Technophilia** — An uncritical enthusiasm for technology and technological solutions that treats innovation as inherently beneficial and resistance as retrograde. Technophilia obscures grief technologies' harms by positioning them as inevitable progress.
- **Thanatechnology** — Technologies specifically designed to manage death, dying, and mourning. The term encompasses both medical technologies that prolong life and digital technologies that reshape practices surrounding death.
- **Therapeutic Justification** — The discursive strategy of legitimising commercial services by claiming they provide psychological or emotional benefits. Grief platforms use therapeutic justifications to position profit extraction as care provision.
- **Uncanny Valley** — The unsettling response humans experience when encountering nearly but not quite human simulations. Griefbots often fall into the uncanny valley, creating discomfort while attempting to replicate deceased persons.

Index

About the Author

William G. Feighery, PhD, is a critical theorist who draws on Foucauldian frameworks to examine contemporary social and political issues. His interdisciplinary research incorporates cross-cultural perspectives, with a focus on post-structuralist theory and continental philosophy.